Education and the Presidency

Lexington Books Politics of Education Series
Frederick M. Wirt, Editor

Michael W. Kirst, Ed., *State, School, and Policitcs: Research Directions*

Joel S. Berke, Michael W. Kirst, *Federal Aid to Education: Who Benefits? Who Governs?*

Al J. Smith, Anthony Downs, M. Leanne Lachman, *Achieving Effective Desegregation*

Kern Alexander, K. Forbis Jordan, *Constitutional Reform of School Finance*

George R. LaNoue, Bruce L.R. Smith, *The Politics of School Decentralization*

David J. Kirby, T. Robert Harris, Robert L. Crain, Christine H. Rossell, *Political Strategies in Northern School Desegregation*

Philip K. Piele, John Stuart Hall, *Budgets, Bonds, and Ballots: Voting Behavior in School Financial Elections*

John C. Hogan, *The Schools, the Courts, and the Public Interest*

Jerome T. Murphy, *State Education Agencies and Discretionary Funds: Grease The Squeaky Wheel*

Howard Hamilton, Sylvan Cohen, *Policy-Making by Plebiscite: School Referenda*

Daniel J. Sullivan, *Public Aid to Nonpublic Schools*

James Hottois, Neal A. Milner, *The Sex Education Controversy: A Study of Politics, Education, and Morality*

Lauriston R. King. *The Washington Lobbyists for Higher Education*

Frederick M. Wirt, Ed., *The Polity of the School: New Research in Educational Politics*

Peter J. Cistone, Ed., *Understanding School Boards: Problems and Prospects*

Lawrence E. Gladieux, Thomas R. Wolanin, *Congress and the Colleges: The National Politics of Higher Education*

Dale Mann, *The Politics of Administrative Representation: School Administrators and Local Democracy*

Harrell R. Rodgers, Jr., Charles S. Bullock III, *Coercion to Compliance*

Richard A. Dershimer, *The Federal Government and Educational R&D*

Tyll van Geel, *Authority to Control the School Program*

Andrew Fishel, Janice Pottker, *National Politics and Sex Discrimination in Education*

Chester E. Finn, Jr., *Education and the Presidency*

Education and
the Presidency

WITHDRAWN

Chester E. Finn, Jr.

with a Foreword by
Daniel P. Moynihan

Lexington Books
D.C. Heath and Company
Lexington, Massachusetts
Toronto

Library of Congress Cataloging in Publication Data

Finn, Chester Evans, Jr.
  Education and the Presidency.

  Includes index.
  1. Education and State—United States. 2. Federal aid to education—
United States. 3. United States—Politics and government—1969-1974. I.
Title.
LC89.F56   379.73   75-32871
ISBN 0-669-00365-4

Published simultaneously in Canada.

Printed in the United States of America.

International Standard Book Number: 0-669-00365-4

Library of Congress Catalog Card Number: 75-32871

288862

In Loving Memory of
Samuel L. Finn,
1890-1976

Contents

Foreword

On April 20, 1977, in the first year of his term, President Jimmy Carter delivered to Congress a message containing a vast set of proposals dealing with the nation's energy resources and their use. For several days the press undertook, without notable success, to describe just what these proposals were. By the weekend they more or less abandoned this effort and directed their attention instead to the question of how the message was assembled in the first place.

The New York Times, on its front page, collated the work of no fewer than seven of its most distinguished Washington correspondents to report that "The plan was conceived in secrecy by technicians, challenged in haste by economists and altered belatedly by politicians. The method may offer some insight into the style and character of an unorthodox President." The message, the headline stated, has been compiled "WITH DISREGARD FOR POLITICS."

The account of *The Washington Post* was not different in the essentials that a political scientist would look for. Its headline read "THE BIRTH OF A POLICY." The story began, "President Carter's energy program is the product of intense secretive work by a tight circle of officials who drew heavily on ideas and statistical models inherited from the Ford and Nixon administrations, according to those involved."

These and a score of other journals did their best to reconstruct the events that had led to the first major domestic policy initiative of the new administration. The reporters would be the first to declare the limitations of their work. They had had a few months' notice that something was going to happen; two or three days to explain what. It is not too much to suggest that the next time—the Next President, for these events are relatively rare in any administration—the next time they will have the benefit of Chester E. Finn, Jr.'s exceptionally lucid, clarifying, and readily understood account of how these things happen.

This may be the first observation to be made about this splendid, small book, and quite the most important. This is a history, to be sure, but it is more than that. It is political science. It describes an important process of American government, the crafting of a presidential message, in terms that capture, or so I believe, some of the uniformities, some of the regularities of the process. I will not say rules, much less laws. That level of confidence we have not yet attained, and may never do. But if you would wish to understand how Jimmy Carter's energy message of April 1977 got put together, you would do very well indeed to read this account of how Richard Nixon's two education messages of March 1970 were assembled.

There is history here as well, and there will hopefully be some who are interested on that account. The two presidential messages which Finn describes provided the basic ideas of the Education Amendments of 1972, which, as I write, are the last significant congressional enactments in this field. They were scarcely small events. In the history of American education policy, they rank with the Morrill Act of 1862, the Federal Vocational Education Act of 1917, the Servicemen's Readjustment Act of 1944 (which established the "G.I. Bill"), the National Defense Education Act of 1958, and the Elementary and Secondary Education Act of 1965.

More importantly, they represent and embody a coming of age of education policy as an aspect of national social policy. Many will differ with the general thrust of the proposals, and presumedly most everyone will find some detail to quarrel with. But the reader would do well to ask whether it is not the case that the two presidential messages that emerged from this process were not the most comprehensive and credible statements of their kind ever to have been sent to the Congress. That, assuredly, is a large proposition, and I pose it only as a query. But what, then, is the contrary evidence? And have any comparable messages been sent since? Is any in prospect? My purpose is merely to suggest that a considerable work of statecraft was involved here: for good or ill, a large initiative. It was addressed, moreover, to a subject of the very first *political* concern at the time. This will perhaps require a measure of imaginative effort for many readers. Education? At the top of the agenda of issues that most concern the American public? Well, yes. In these months—two to three years, really— education issues for once had seized the public mind and the subject became political as it had scarcely ever been before and has not been since. This book, to repeat, evokes that period and describes the response of the executive branch of the national government. Political scientists and educators alike will find the subject compelling.

As one who was involved in these events, I found two particularly absorbing themes running through the narrative. How does a president deal with information he has, and most others do not have? How does a president, as the leader of the national government, restrain the expansion of the powers of government?

The first question arose with respect to the message on elementary and secondary education. Put plainly, by 1969 social science research had pretty much established that the educational theory on which almost all previous federal education legislation had been based—was wrong. Many will find that put *too* plainly, but I do not see an alternative. Evidence to this effect had been accumulating in small research programs for some time and then was massively confirmed by the study associated with James S. Coleman in the mid-1960s. It fell to me to organize a faculty seminar at Harvard University to pour over the Coleman findings, which was done and which in the end only confirmed them. The result was one of those moments in the history of science. A relatively small number of people knew that what most people thought was wrong. As Finn writes, the president's program "rhetorically assaulted the school establishment itself, and did so in the name of a theory—more precisely a body of data—that probably fewer than a thousand people in the nation understood at the time."

Let us note that nothing since has disproven the data. To the contrary, it is scarcely any longer contested. And yet it is still in measure an arcane proposition—that education resources have but little bearing on education results—and so also is the public policy that is seemingly dictated by this finding, which is that it is results, not resources, that must be the measure of public policy. But I leave it to the reader to pursue.

And then there is the matter, of which Schumpeter spoke years ago, of the conquest of the private sector by the public sector—a process he thought to be endemic to liberal society, and which he very much feared would end with the demise of liberalism. In this long, purportedly inexorable process, the events described in this book are not of the greatest order; and yet how they grasp the imagination. It was a moment of high tension between the national government and the nation's leading universities. There had never before been such a moment. Congress, increasingly, saw the universities as undeserving and threatening and meriting reprisal on grounds that national policy could not go forward until they changed their self-disruptive behavior. The universities replied that they would never change their self-disruptive behavior until Congress (and the president) changed national policy. (See the Amherst Declaration of April 1969.) The presidency, in between, sought to restrain any action by Congress and sought even more assertively to persuade the universities that they must never let the conduct of their internal affairs become a dependent variable, to use a favored university term, of American foreign policy or American any-kind-of-policy. The president's message pleaded with the Congress: "to intervene to impose freedom, is by definition to suppress it." It appealed to the campuses: the great need was "for the Federal government to help academic communities to pursue excellence and reform in fields of their own choosing . . . and by means of their own choice." From the very first, the universities, through their various organizations, rejected this counsel and spurned the legislation that embodied it, notably a National Foundation for Higher Education whose purpose would have been to provide funds to higher education free of federal purpose. Almost alone of the many proposals sent to Congress in March 1970, this did not become law. The representatives of higher education fair to insisted on continuing the specialized, fragmented aid programs that the presidency had assured them were leading to their ever-greater dependence on the federal government and ever-greater federal intervention in their affairs.

By mid-decade the presidents of some of the larger universities seemingly awoke to what was happening, and speeches began to be reported deploring the ever-greater federal intervention in university affairs. But it was, for this period at all events, too late. No one was listening. Or those who listened responded with a not altogether attractive display of *schadenfreude:* Were not the universities getting what they had prescribed for others?

Robert H. Bork has written of this aftermath in a poignant mood. He cites Walter Bagehot:

The characteristic danger of great nations, like the Romans and the English, which have a long history of continuous creation, is that they may at last fail from not comprehending the great institutions which they have created.

He cites Robert Nisbet on the decline of authority and autonomy in our time, "the twilight of authority." And then Bork writes:

It is as though over the past few years the American institutional landscape has been flattened.

... [T]he autonomy and self-governing capacity of universities are now so little thought of that not only legislatures and federal agencies but courts are willing as never before in our history to scrutinize every exercise of discretion.

How can this have come to pass? Most of all, Bork suggests and we would all agree, because higher education is dependent as never before on federal money. Now this was, perhaps, inevitable. But was it equally inevitable that dependence would have been accompanied by the detailed control that is so increasingly in evidence? I don't suppose that anyone could say for certain. But Chester Finn has written an enlightening book that describes the effort by one group of presidential aides to avoid this outcome. Their failure in this one respect, contrasted with their overall success, seems to me to raise quite the largest issues of public policy in America today.

Daniel P. Moynihan

May 1977
Washington, D.C.

Introduction

The final months of Richard Nixon's tenure at the White House still evoke such emotion that a balanced appraisal of his entire administration must await the attention of future historians. Yet it is not premature to recall that the sixty-six months of his presidency embraced much more than the antecedents and aftermath of Watergate. There was also a time, perhaps two years or a bit more, between his inauguration in early 1969 and the appearance of the Pentagon Papers in the spring of 1971, when the men and women who worked for him may fairly be said to have taken part in a serious effort to rationalize and reform many of the domestic policies of the American national government.

Parts of that attempt were ill conceived, and parts were poorly executed. Some of the participants thought they had the nation's best interests at heart; others were looking out for the president; still others trusted that the two were not incompatible. Republican ideology, such as it is, animated some of their undertakings; a nonpartisan vision of social policy beheld others. Of the two boldest initiatives—revenue sharing and a guaranteed income plan—one passed Congress and got underway while the other perished in the Senate, the victim of an extraordinary alliance of liberals and conservatives.

Important realms of domestic policy such as health and housing got scant attention during this time. Others—arts and humanities, the environment— received more than ever before. Always in the background was foreign affairs, every president's preoccupation. Nothing on the domestic front could long distract Nixon from the travail of Indochina, the opening to Peking, the stirrings of detente with the Soviet Union, and the intractable dilemmas of the Middle East. But in the Executive Office and in the principal government agencies was a sizable group of men and women—some creatures of this administration, others civil servants of long tenure—whose mandate was domestic policy and whose mission, whether at the president's behest or on their own initiative, was to do what they could to devise a reasonable match between the needs of the society, the capacities of the federal government, the programs they had inherited, and the philosophical and political foundations of the new administration.

This is the tale of one such group, the people who worked on education policy, and of their activities in 1969 and 1970 as they formulated the ideas that would frame the executive branch's conception of the federal role in the nation's educational enterprise and as they designed the proposals that would serve as script for that role.

To assert that these were extraordinarily able, tireless, and creative individuals does them scant justice, while inviting disbelief from an audience conditioned by subsequent "White House horrors" to assume the worst of all who labored on behalf of Richard Nixon. Yet without downplaying the later scandals that would lead to the disgraced president's resignation, it is also useful to assist the spotlight of history to illuminate the early years of the Nixon presidency, the period William Safire terms "before the fall." For it was an important time in the development of federal domestic policy, not least in the field of education; it provides an interesting case study of presidential policy making; and it lends itself to reflection on how that process might be improved.

In the interests of full disclosure, the author's own part in these proceedings needs to be spelled out. In early 1969, I came to the White House to join the staff of the new Council on Urban Affairs and its executive secretary, Daniel P. Moynihan, who had been my faculty adviser at the Harvard Graduate School of Education. I stayed for two years, serving on Moynihan's staff until Nixon reorganized the White House domestic policy apparatus in late 1969, whereupon I was invited to join John Ehrlichman's much-enlarged staff. I did so, stipulating that I would also continue assisting Moynihan when he wanted me to. And I asked to keep working primarily on education policy, both because I was interested in it and because Harvard had agreed to allow me to complete my doctorate by doing a "thesis project" on presidential education policy making.

This meant I was assigned to assist Edward L. Morgan, the Ehrlichman deputy in charge of human resource programs and chairman of the two "working groups" created to finish the education policy development process that the Urban Affairs Council had begun. In my remaining fifteen months at the White House, then, I spent most of my time collaborating with Morgan (on education and other subjects in his purview) and the balance aiding Moynihan, who also continued to supervise my graduate school progress. Since education policy remained a topic of active interest to him and since he was a charter member of both working groups, my dual loyalties occasionally cast me in the peculiar role of an aide asked by one boss to draft a response to a proposal I had ghosted for the other, but the fondness and mutual respect Morgan and Moynihan held for each other made this potentially awkward situation more stimulating than troublesome.

As the working groups' "recording secretary" and chief of staff, I took part in all their meetings, prepared many of the memoranda and drafts that they considered, and collaborated with individual members and their aides. It was a demanding and heady but enthralling experience for a young graduate student, and one I heartily recommend, notwithstanding the Watergate-induced advice of other White House alumni that none but seasoned hands should enter the presidential orbit. Although the intervening years have lent some perspective to my contributions as a "Staff Assistant to the President," it is a lasting source of pride to turn to the two education policy messages that Richard Nixon sent to Congress in March 1970 (both reprinted in the Appendix) and find there a few ideas and more than a few paragraphs that emerged from my typewriter.

The biases of a participant unavoidably color the following pages, but I was an observer as well, for my Harvard assignment obliged me to keep a journal for monthly submission to a faculty committee in Cambridge and, in the spring of

1970, to pen an analysis of what I had seen and done. Those journals and analysis (both now accessible in unexpurgated form at the Gutman Library of the Harvard Graduate School of Education) provide the primary sources for this volume. In addition, I retained file copies of many of the papers prepared by or submitted to the education working groups, and most of the unreferenced quotations in this book (particularly Chapters 3 and 4, the "case studies") are drawn from those materials.

My heavy intellectual and personal debts cannot adequately be discharged in a brief acknowledgement. Daniel P. Moynihan, long time friend and mentor as well as employer and professor, made it possible for me to be a graduate student as well as a White House staffer, and later encouraged me to assay this book, for which he has graciously provided the Foreword. Stephen Hess, his deputy at the White House and more recently my colleague at the Brookings Institution, was patient, supportive, and insightful both in the doing and in the retelling. John Ehrlichman readily agreed to all my personal requests, including the unusual procedure of sharing with a panel of university faculty members the events that transpired in the White House each month. Edward L. Morgan did more than tolerate an aide he had not previously known; he was also a much-needed defender, splendid supervisor, and firm friend. Jean Frayer was one of those legendary White House secretaries, selfless, tireless, and good-humored even with a boss who was her junior and who kept asking her to type the reports of a graduate student along with the official papers of a president. Although that president barely knew I existed, it goes without saying—but should be said anyway—that were it not for Richard Nixon, none of this would have been possible.

At Harvard, Francis H. Duehay smoothed the path for an unconventional doctoral project and amiably kept the pressure on an aberrant graduate student whose project kept getting redefined and who was frequently tardy in meeting his academic commitments. As a member of my faculty committee, Walter McCann subordinated his personal views about the administration I served to an informed and helpful interest in my progress. Theodore R. Sizer, then Dean of the Graduate School of Education, was supportive and encouraging throughout.

In writing this book, I have been the grateful recipient of informed criticism and thoughtful suggestions from Stephen Hess, Gregory Anrig, Richard P. Nathan, Frederick M. Wirt, and Daniel P. Moynihan. Caroletta Tresvant, Radmila Nikolic, Celia Rich, and Donna Daniels Verdier provided expert secretarial assistance.

Last in this recital, but first in every other respect, Renu, Arti, and Aloke did more than cheerfully tolerate the late nights and long weekends when "daddy" was busy working on "the Nixon book." They lifted my spirits, brooked no unexcused delays in a much-delayed manuscript, and made coming home a joy.

1

Advising the President

The executive power shall be vested in a President of the United States of America.

          —Article II, Section 1, Constitution of the United States

The president personifies the executive branch of the federal government. He and his vice president alone are answerable to the electorate for its accomplishments and failings. Every action taken in its hundreds of agencies and by its millions of employees is thought to be taken by authority of the power the Constitution vests in him. If the sum of those actions pleases the people, he may be reelected. If it sorely offends the nation, he may be removed from office.

Because he cannot do the job alone, he has obtained vast amounts of help. Others collect the revenues, sign the checks, train the soldiers, control the movements of civil aircraft, manage the laboratories, sweep the floors, purchase the typewriters, and respond to millions of requests from ordinary citizens. So routinized and familiar are most federal government activities that we do not even consciously associate them with the occupant of the Oval Office. To him are reserved far vaguer responsibilities such as leadership, inspiration, direction, and—perhaps the vaguest of all—policy.

Policy directly implicates the president and the presidency, the latter an elusive governmental entity most easily thought of as the combined words, deeds, and responsibilities of several hundred senior executive branch employees appointed to their jobs by the president and several thousand more whose assignments are also linked to his tenure. Although more and more institutionalized in recent years, the presidency remains a direct extension of the president—a durable vessel that can be filled with the people, ideas, and activities of his choosing.

Policy, for our purposes, is the expression of the ideas of the presidency about the conduct of the government.[a] Usually, though not always, it is the formal expression of those ideas in carefully chosen words. It is intended to shape the activities of the federal government at home and abroad and thus also to affect the activities of those in contact with the government, be they ordinary citizens, large corporations, or foreign nations. Because the legislative and

---

[a]Richard Rose favors the terms *political objectives,* which he defines as "the expression of political values in terms that may be realized in the immediately foreseeable future by or through government"; and *goals,* which he construes as statements of political values "that government may realize in the determinate but more distant future." See Richard Rose, *Managing Presidential Objectives* (New York: The Free Press, 1976), p. 2.

1

judicial branches share power with the executive, checking and balancing its actions, the presidency seldom has the last or only word on the conduct of the government. The Founding Fathers saw to that. Presidential policy is just one element, looming larger in some spheres of federal activity than in others and occasionally eclipsed by contrary policies of the Congress or the courts.

Our immediate concern, however, is not with the fate of presidential policy but with its formulation, for the United States has long since passed the era when the president sat down at his desk and crafted his own policies. He still signs his name to the requisite documents—if a machine does not do it for him—and he still utters the words of his speeches, but almost never is he their sole author and often he takes little part in the making of his policies until they are deposited before him for ratification.

Who, then, makes policy for the presidency and how do they make it? Where do the ideas come from? Who decides which among them to select? Who painstakingly crafts the words in which those ideas are expressed?

No rules govern this process and relatively little is known about it, for it is idiosyncratic, often secretive, and seldom open to the public scrutiny that we are accustomed to in congressional hearings and courtroom arguments. Even within the executive branch, we know far more about most other activities than about the process of advising the president and formulating his policies. "Of all the aspects of the Presidency," Cronin and Greenberg wrote in 1969, "this is, to date, the least explored and the least understood."[1]

The past few years have witnessed an outpouring of books about the presidency that range from lurid White House confessionals to scholarly studies of the nature and structure of the presidential enterprise. Even so, surprisingly little is known about the policy-making process itself.

This volume focuses on domestic policy during the early years of the Nixon administration and, in particular, on the sequence of events leading up to the president's signing in March 1970 of two Messages to Congress dealing with federal education policy. Whereas in foreign and military affairs, the president still has extraordinary power to make decisions and take actions, in domestic matters the chief product of presidential policy making is usually a cluster of proposals for congressional review. Unlike a speech, a press conference statement or a letter, in which the president's *views* on a particular subject may be expressed, the Message to Congress asks approval of a specific set of actions and explains why the president thinks them desirable. While the draft legislation accompanying the message provides the basis for formal congressional consideration, it is the message—itself a rather stylized, sometimes pretentious, sometimes eloquent piece of prose—that sets forth the administration's reasoning, explains its intentions, and endeavors to persuade others of its wisdom and sincerity.

Presidents send many Messages to Congress. Although they are not the exclusive vehicle for conveying administration policy, they are a familiar and useful one—establishing a written record of ideas that members of Congress can evaluate, journalists can excerpt and explain, editorialists can judge, interest groups can react to, and the ordinary citizen, should he or she be so inclined, can read and usually understand. Hence the making of a presidential message offers a revealing window on the policy development process.

The preparation of a Message to Congress has both substantive and mechanical aspects. The ideas themselves must come from somewhere, and be evaluated, sharpened, and culled by someone. Then they must be put into suitable presidential language, accompanied by legislation drafted to carry them out and by other official papers and unveiled to the press and the public with appropriate fanfare. The president may entrust both the ideas and their preparation to the same people, or he may divide the tasks.

Although this study does not ignore the mechanical side of message writing—in the Nixon White House the two processes were usually joined—its emphasis is on the substance, the interplay of ideas, analyses, personalities, and procedures that molded the content of the two education messages.

If we assume that presidents must ordinarily get their policy ideas from others, especially about complex subjects they have not personally mastered, the obvious question is whom. Although the potential sources can be combined in a hundred different ways, the basic typology is surprisingly short.

Presidents can rely on their personal advisors in the White House and other parts of the executive office. They can turn to their cabinet officers and other appointees based in the line agencies but still regarded as part of the presidency. They can avail themselves of the government bureaucracy, relying on career professionals who spend their years attending to the particular subject on which the president seeks advice. Or they can go outside the executive branch altogether in search of ideas and recommendations. Outsiders comprise much the largest category, including experts and laymen, interest group spokesmen and disinterested critics, congressmen and journalists, scholars and practitioners, old friends and new acquaintances.

Advisors from any of these categories can be tapped in various ways: as individuals written, phoned, or invited to meet with the president; as working parties or task forces, instructed to assemble ideas into serviceable policy packages; as formal advisory commissions, charged with studying a subject and making recommendations to the president; as White House conferences, in which large gatherings of people mull over a subject or problem in search of guidance for the government.

Every source of advice and configuration of advisors has distinctive advantages for the president, and if they had no drawbacks, he would presumably want to use all of them. But each has its costs, too, and these tend to multiply as the number of people and advisory mechanisms increases. The principal costs are delay, dissension, and unwanted publicity. Presidents are usually in a hurry to set forth their new proposals, and every additional person asked to participate in the policy development process is apt to make it take longer. Similarly, large numbers of advisors, particularly if assembled in more than one forum, are more likely to disagree with one another, and the harder the president tries for broad-based or "representative" counsel, the surer he is to elicit conflicting recommendations. That is fine, if he is prepared personally to mediate among his various advisors, to expose himself to dispute, and to make hard choices under pressure. Those may be thought normal, even commendable presidential tasks, but it is not to be wondered that he may prefer to consider unanimous recommendations prepared by a harmonious group of trusted counselors and to avoid tough conciliation sessions.

As for secrecy, it is not nearly so important in domestic as in international affairs, but there is some political and public relations value in surprise, even when the subject is as familiar as education. A presidential policy pronouncement stands a better chance of winning headlines if his proposals have not previously been aired publicly, and he is more likely to win plaudits for a medium-sized program if his audience knows nothing of the grandiose one that some of his advisors urged. Although restricting the number of participants does not assure confidentiality, the larger the group and the more outsiders it contains, the likelier its recommendations are to leak. And leaks give the president's opponents more opportunity to sharpen their knives and position themselves to flay his proposals.

Thus organizing a presidential policy-making process is itself an exercise in balancing rival values. One cannot have both leisure and speed, openness and confidentiality, creativity and discipline, participation and unanimity. Not surprisingly, therefore, presidents have built their advice-gathering and policy-making machinery in many different ways, engineering it to their personal styles, to their political beliefs, to the nature and significance of the subject at hand, to the organization chart and management practices of the particular administration, to the personalities and predilections of their chief advisors, and even to the phase of their term in office (for practices well-suited to the aftermath of an election may not be as satisfactory just before the next one). The goal that the president seeks will also influence the process that he chooses; if he earnestly wishes his proposals to pass Congress, he may have them developed quite differently than if his main intent is simply to communicate a viewpoint to the public. Winning favor with a particular interest group or constituency may likewise call for a different process than appealing to the ordinary citizen.

Perhaps the strongest variable is the president's own political temperament, for it determines his choice of advisors, his preferred *modus operandi*, the slant of his own views on the subject at hand, the kinds of constraints placed on those who develop policy for him, the extent of his own involvement, and his receptivity to others' ideas. Arthur M. Schlesinger, Jr. argues that "contention" is an "indispensable means of government," and that "above all [the president] must not make himself the prisoner of a single information system."[2] But a chief executive who prefers to shield himself from conflict and to avoid the tensions inherent in multiple channels of advice may design or let others design for him a monolithic advisory system that forms messy ideas into neat policies without himself having to referee the contest.

If one were to point to a single great divide that sets one sort of advisory process apart from another, it would be the choice between primary reliance on loyalists or on outsiders—that is, between the presidency and everybody else. While most presidents give the appearance of doing both, the existence of a well-publicized panel of eminent citizens does not mean that the president's policy will be affected one whit by its opinions. The outsiders may simply be window-dressing. Worse, from the president's standpoint, they may cause him trouble if the content of their unheeded counsel gets into the public domain, there to be used by critics as a gauge against which the president's policies may be found wanting. It is difficult to impose on outside advisors the stern discipline that presidential appointees take for granted. Hence the involvement of persons outside the president's official family poses some risks.

At the same time, a president can make adroit use of outsiders if he wishes to, provided he chooses them carefully and handles them deftly. They bring potential assets to the policy development process that the president's own appointees may lack. They can supply varied and creative ideas about what the government ought to do from the perspective of observers, experts, or consumers of federal programs rather than suppliers. They can help the president estimate in advance the reactions to potential policies of various interest groups whose support or hostility will affect the fate both of the policies and of the president espousing them. And if the outside advisors themselves endorse the president's proposals, whether because they genuinely favor the ideas or because cooptation has stilled their opposition, they can sway the views of others.

Outsiders may influence policy development in many ways, sometimes without knowing it. The president's own appointees, themselves quondam outsiders now doing a stint in government, will most likely draw ideas from the teachings, writings, and personal counsel of others whom they respect. Individuals and interest groups who know that a policy domain important to them is about to be reviewed by the presidency will not hesitate to communicate their views via private and public channels. Early signals from the White House or the agencies will prompt letters, editorials, phone calls, and personal visits. But modern presidents have also tended to make heavier use of formal structures for involving outsiders. Where Harry Truman appointed an average of 2.5 presidential advisory commissions a year, John Kennedy named 4.2 such panels per annum, Lyndon Johnson 5.4, and Richard Nixon averaged 8.3 during the years of his first term. (Eisenhower, an aberration in this pattern, designated just 9 commissions during his entire eight years.[3])

Although Thomas Wolanin judges that two thirds of the 99 presidential advisory commissions between 1945 and 1972 won "at least some substantial implementation of their recommendations," one can nevertheless detect large gaps between the frequency with which presidents create such panels and the influence of outside advice on presidential policy making.[4] We might suppose, for example, that Nixon's seeming devotion to advisory commissions—he named 33 of them in four years—indicated a high degree of receptivity to such advice.[b] While that may have been so in other facets of his presidency, the following pages show that the development of his education policy was heavily weighted toward his own appointees. Indeed, the preparation of Nixon's March 1970 Message to Congress represents the virtual apotheosis of a policy development process that could fairly be termed the opposite of the outside advisory commission. Education policy in the Nixon White House flowed into the Oval Office from a pair of "working groups" drawn entirely from the Nixon presidency. Chaired by a presidential assistant and comprised primarily of other appointees, the few federal careerists participating in them were drawn from the Executive Office of the President and took part only as aides to the political appointees for whom they worked.

Interagency task forces are common in Washington, and all presidents employ high level panels of that genre from time to time to help shape administration policy. Often invisible to the public, they are invaluable to the chief executive as an efficient means of concentrating energy and intelligence on complex policy domains that need to be examined from multiple perspectives before he selects a course of action.

The working groups so characteristic of domestic policy development in the early years of the Nixon administration did not differ in kind from a hundred task forces before and since, but several differences of degree are manifest in the following pages. First, the president relied heavily if not exclusively on them as sources of information and advice. He allowed them to define the problems, frame the options, recommend particular courses of action, and prepare the words in which those policies would be expressed. He did not reach out for conflicting advice or avail himself of other information sources. Second, the working groups systematically excluded persons with conflicting loyalties or values who might not put the president's interests first. They rarely solicited the views of career employees running existing government programs, outside experts and interest groups, or members of Congress and their staffs. Third, the working groups were firmly rooted in the White House and were thus an

---

[b]Wolanin employs a strict and formal definition of a presidential advisory commission and omits a number of panels and task forces of various sorts that fail to meet his criteria. For example, President Johnson's 1964 Task Force on Education, chaired by John Gardner, which by most accounts played a large role in the design of the Great Society's education programs, is omitted because neither its membership nor its report was made public. Similarly, the transition task force headed by Alan Pifer, which advised Richard Nixon on education policy failed of inclusion on several counts, not least the fact that Nixon had not yet assumed the presidency at the time when he formed it. But for those commissions he acknowledges, Wolanin is rather more generous in his definition of what constitutes success and impact. See Thomas R. Wolanin, *Presidential Advisory Commissions* (Madison: University of Wisconsin Press, 1975).

extrapolation of the president's own staff structure rather than an extension of his cabinet. Although senior agency officials took active part in them, it was clear to all that they reported to the president through his top personal advisors rather than through the heads of his line agencies. Fourth, while not secret, the working groups were secretive. Having but one client, they had no reason to talk to anyone else about what they were thinking.

Chapter 2 prepares the stage on which the education working groups were to perform by sketching the condition of American education at the time of Nixon's inauguration, introducing the main actors, examining the new administration's earliest statements about education, and tracing the design of the domestic policy machinery that created the working groups.

The third and fourth chapters are case studies of the evolution of the two presidential messages: the first on elementary and secondary education, the second on higher education.

Chapter 5 summarizes the fate of the policies Nixon proposed in 1970 and locates them in the changing landscape of federal involvement with education.

In the concluding chapter, we return to the perspective of the presidency and look back at the subject of education in an effort to understand why it receives the kinds of attention that it gets at the White House and to speculate on some alternatives.

Stirrings and Startings

The Condition of Education

Richard Nixon's election did not occur at a happy time for American education. Although total enrollments were the largest ever, the declining birthrate was just beginning to erode the elementary school population, and it was clear that the effects would soon be felt in high schools and colleges, thereby putting an end to two decades of steady growth in every part of the nation's instructional enterprise. A system that had struggled with marked success to accommodate swelling student hordes was ill prepared for an era in which dwindling classes would negate the best argument for bigger budgets, in which teachers and professors—still pouring out of the graduate schools in record numbers—would be a surplus commodity rather than a scarce resource, and in which new courses and programs would dictate the elimination of old ones.

Urban schools were widely held to be in a state of crisis. A week before inauguration day, the *Saturday Review* published a symposium on "Education in the Ghetto" organized by the Committee for Economic Development to highlight the fact that "the schooling of deprived minorities" had been "a tragic failure."[1] Notwithstanding a national commitment to compensatory education that had poured billions of dollars through the Economic Opportunity Act and the Elementary and Secondary Education Act, the summer fires that burned from California's Watts in 1965 across the land to Washington's 14th and U streets in 1968 had a profound impact on the society and those concerned with its schools. "The ghetto poor," wrote New Orleans Superintendent Carl Dolce, "are becoming poorer, and most educational institutions are failing to provide their children with instruction that relates to their present condition."[2]

Community control was also in the air. "The black community," explained District of Columbia school principal Kenneth W. Haskins, "has decided that it has to make the decisions about what can and cannot be tolerated for its children because society as a whole has largely failed the black community in this respect."[3] The disastrous clash between such conviction and the education establishment that would erupt in Ocean Hill-Brownsville and elsewhere was foreshadowed in Albert Shanker's retort that, "There is nothing more dangerous than turning to the poor in the ghetto for some massive answer."[4]

Yet the compensatory programs that Shanker and others touted as a solution to the urban school problem and as a cure for the educational ills of disadvantaged students were themselves already coming into question. The

9

massive study of educational inequality known as the Coleman Report had appeared in 1966 with its conclusion, barely understood at first, that the schools themselves have less effect on what children learn, at least compared to other factors beyond the schools' reach, than the nation had assumed since the days of Horace Mann. What then the hope for compensatory education if the variation between schools had scant correlation with their students' achievement scores?

In the colleges, for the time being, enrollments still soared. The autumn of Nixon's election they were half a million larger than the year before. But campus unrest was spreading, from Berkeley in the mid-sixties to Columbia in the spring of 1968, and the American university was fast losing its sanctity. In the summer of 1968—the season when the Democrats' nomination of Hubert Humphrey in Chicago was accompanied by nationally televised street battles between Mayor Daley's police and angry youths who were widely, if imprecisely, depicted as college students—Nathan Glazer wrote:

In the universities, participatory democracy has now been replaced by a new doctrine which decrees that when democratic procedures either do not exist (as indeed they do not in many sectors of many universities) or when a democratic system fails to respond to deeply felt needs (as with the Vietnam war) then it is quite legitimate to engage in disruption and disorder to bring about change.[5]

At the end of the 1968-69 school year, the American Council on Education estimated that 145 campuses had experienced "violent" protest and 524 were host to "disruptive" protest in those two semesters spanning the end of the Johnson administration and the beginning of the Nixon presidency.[6] Yet despite the turmoil behind the ivied walls, higher education leaders unabashedly levied their claims on the nation for greater resources. A few weeks before inauguration day, the Carnegie Commission on Higher Education issued its initial recommendations, calling on Washington to hike the federal share of financial support for postsecondary institutions from one-fifth to one-third of the total—a move that would increase the government contribution from $4 billion to $13 billion per annum within eight years.[7]

That the enrollment boom which gave rise to these demands could not last seemed irrelevant. Demographic projections that showed an eventual levelling, then an absolute decline in the eighteen- to twenty-four-year-old population fired few imaginations in a higher education community still struggling to house those seeking admission. The academy confidently assumed that the proportion of eager students in each succeeding high school generation would continue to rise and that new clienteles—older people, minorities, women—would more than offset any shrinkage in the age group traditionally supplying most of the freshman class.

In the late sixties, the costs of higher education were rising even faster than its enrollments, especially in private institutions, and some schools found red ink in their balance sheets. In one sample of forty-eight private colleges, half showed operating deficits in fiscal 1969, though their tuitions had soared.[8] Additional income was needed—or costs would have to decline—and the states showed little disposition to aid their private colleges. The volatile condition of the campuses scarcely encouraged greater voluntary support—alumni giving was to fall for the first time in memory between 1968 and 1969—and Washington seemed the only alternative.

The other great distress in American education in 1968 was the enduring problem of racial segregation. The Southern Regional Council issued a special report entitled "Lawlessness and Disorder: Fourteen Years of Failure in Southern School Desegregation," which argued that since the Supreme Court's 1954 *Brown* decision, there had been little progress in complying with its requirements, indeed that more Negro youngsters studied in segregated southern schools in the mid-sixties than when the Court ruled. Ninety-six percent of Mississippi's black students attended such schools in September 1967, 95 percent in Alabama, 94 percent in South Carolina.

What in the fifties was chiefly a concern of the judiciary had, with the passage of civil rights legislation in the sixties, become a matter of immediate concern to the executive branch and the Congress, as the requirement that federal funds must not be given to segregated school systems began to take hold. Enforcing this provision had embroiled Washington in a divisive and ugly sequence, particularly as "freedom-of-choice plans" were struck down by the courts and as busing—in many instances the only feasible way to effect school integration where residential patterns were segregated—came to be seen as a death sentence for the "neighborhood school." In 1967, Congress stipulated that HEW must apply its desegregation guidelines uniformly in northern and southern states, and suddenly the political impact of school integration took on national significance, at a time when rising black consciousness and the demand for community control also meant that federal enforcement of desegregation requirements was losing its constituency among many who might have been thought its primary beneficiaries.

Lyndon Johnson's desire to be remembered as the "education president" had led to landmark legislation with great consequence for the nation's schools and colleges: the Economic Opportunity Act of 1964, the Civil Rights Act of 1964, the Higher Education Act of 1965, and the Elementary and Secondary Education Act of 1965. Federal outlays for education approximately tripled from $3.1 billion to $9 billion during the fiscal years spanned by the Johnson administration. If he had not put them permanently to rest, he had at least picked his way around the two historic obstacles to federal education aid: the fear of federal control and the church-state issue. With skillful assistance from HEW Secretary John Gardner and Education Commissioners Francis Keppel and Harold Howe II, and with S. Douglass Cater, Jr. working behind the scenes from his office in the White House basement, Johnson had enticed Congress into a momentous extension of federal responsibility for the nation's educational enterprise.

The basic governance arrangements were unchanged. Control remained with the states, as the Tenth Amendment stipulated, and authority was customarily delegated by them to local school boards and college trustees. But the enlargement of the federal financial commitment and the numerous strings attached to the new programs meant that in practice Washington had become a partner, albeit a limited one, in the nation's educational system.

As the Vietnam War ate into resources that might otherwise have gone to the domestic programs of the Great Society, and as mounting unease with that conflict showed up in campus protests and in heightened mistrust between the White House and the education community, a chill set in. John Gardner's well-publicized resignation in January 1968 symbolized the frustration that had overtaken hope in the few short years since President Johnson had flown to Stonewall, Texas, to sign Public Law 89-10 outside the one-room schoolhouse where he had studied as a boy. Although the governmentwide dollar total for education continued to rise, outlays by the Office of Education actually declined in the last year (fiscal 1969) of the Johnson administration. Federal funds for colleges and universities—primarily for research—which had more than doubled between 1963 and 1968 rose only a bit in 1969 and, under the fiscal 1970 budget that Johnson bequeathed his successor, would fall by $227 million.

The mood deteriorated, too. The education president was denounced by educators. The man who had channeled vast sums to the nation's colleges and universities could not find a campus where he was welcome to give a speech. Radical student groups came under federal surveillance. The White House, dominated by a president who did not want to hear bad news, hunkered down and listened to few of the academics eager to advise it.

In education policy, the presidency had surrendered the initiative to the Congress, which as the decade ebbed was less concerned with new legislation than with the sums to be appropriated for existing programs. Three months after Johnson left office, a group of education associations banded together to form a new lobbying arm called the Emergency Committee for Full Funding of Education Programs. It was a response to what they deemed a niggardly allocation to education in the fiscal 1970 budget that was submitted in the closing days of the outgoing administration. The purpose of the Full Funding Committee was to persuade Congress to boost these sums, and it proved extraordinarily successful, ultimately getting $1.3 billion added on Capitol Hill. Although this drama would not reach its finale until early 1970, when Nixon's veto of the inflated and belated appropriation would be sustained, by mid-1969 the principal education debate taking place along the shores of the Potomac centered on dollars, not policies. And by then it was easy to forget that Lyndon Johnson, the education president, had authored the disputed budget, for his successor showed no interest in enlarging its numbers. In August, Nixon would announce his refusal to spend any more on education in fiscal 1970 and by posing the contrast between a Democratic Congress that favored spending more and a Republican administration that insisted on holding a lid on the amounts, caused lines to be drawn that would extend well into subsequent deliberations on the content of federal education policy.

New Faces in the White House

Nothing in Richard Nixon's record encouraged educators to suppose that his inauguration would improve matters. A red-baiter as congressman, as vice president (and soon-to-be presidential candidate) in 1960 he had cast the deciding vote against a Senate amendment that would direct federal funds into school construction and teacher salaries.

During the 1968 campaign, one speechwriter later recalled, candidate Nixon told his staff that "I'm a nut on education. Balance the budget on a lot of things, but when it comes to education, I'm a nut about it."[9] But this "nuttiness" was largely concealed from the voters. He did make one major campaign address on the subject of education, two weeks before election day, and he did "pledge [that] my Administration [will] be second to none in its concern for education."[10] But he stressed the mechanism of "bloc grants" as the safest way to insure that control would remain in state and local hands. And he insisted that nonpublic schools also participate in federal programs. While both propositions were defensible in their own right, in the context of 1968 both could also be interpreted as signals that, under a Nixon presidency, Washington would back away from the categorical programs that characterized federal education policy and also from the civil rights enforcement that accompanied such programs.[a]

For higher education, the candidate urged federal student loans and tax credits, with the balance of needed support left to private, state, and local sources. He acknowledged the singular plight of private colleges, but offered as a solution only "special tax advantages for donations" to them. He inveighed against "permissiveness" in the classroom and associated himself with moves to deny federal aid to disruptive students. He saluted the neighborhood school, endorsed job-related education, proposed a National Teacher Corps (although the Teacher Corps had been around since 1965), and recommended a National Institute for the Educational Future to "take us into the space age in education."[11]

The Republicans had come some distance from 1964, when the party nominated a candidate whose opposition to federal education aid was legendary and who spearheaded much of the opposition the Johnson programs later faced in the Senate. But in light of the differences in legislation on the books in 1964 and 1968, candidate Nixon's program appeared hardly more ambitious than Goldwater's had been.

---

[a]It should be recalled that "nonpublic schools" in 1968 no longer referred exclusively to church-related institutions and elite private campuses, since so-called "segregation academies" were appearing in some districts faced with integration of their public schools.

Interest groups and lobbyists naturally form their first impressions of a new administration from the appointments the president makes to positions with influence over the programs and policies that affect them. By this criterion, Nixon's initial choices were a mixed bag. Within the White House staff itself, three professors—Arthur Burns, Henry Kissinger, and Daniel P. Moynihan—assumed prominent positions. Two were engaged with domestic policy and one of these, Harvard's Moynihan, had actually been a professor of *education*. But his deep immersion in the Coleman data, on which he was one of the nation's foremost authorities, had turned him into something of an agnostic toward the doctrine of simply spending more money as an answer to the needs of disadvantaged students. More social scientist than educationist when he moved into Cater's old office in the West Wing basement, Moynihan wanted to examine the research and weigh the evidence before urging any policy direction on the president. Moreover, his clear priority—for presidential attention, for White House energies, for additional resources—in 1969 was, as it had been for half a decade, finding a solution to the worsening problems of a welfare system that fractured the families it was intended to sustain.

Counselor Burns said little about education. His primary concern was economic policy. But he brought onto his staff one scholar, Roger A. Freeman from Stanford's Hoover Institution, who ranked among the most outspoken opponents of federal spending on education, save through the mechanism of tax credits, an idea that—because it benefited the wealthy more than the poor and required high tuition levels to benefit anyone very much—had long been abhorrent to liberals in general and to supporters of public schools and low-tuition state colleges in particular.

Elsewhere in the Executive Office of the President, Nixon placed well-known academics in the traditional slots of Science Advisor (Cal Tech's Lee DuBridge) and the Council of Economic Advisors. As director of the Office of Economic Opportunity he appointed Congressman Donald Rumsfeld, who turned out to be more moderate in the executive branch than his suburban Chicago constituency had found him to be on Capitol Hill, but whose name hardly inspired an OEO clientele that remembered Sargent Shriver.

Similarly, the new secretary of Health, Education and Welfare, California's Robert Finch, was a moderate-to-liberal Republican, but a relative unknown to an education fraternity that had once enjoyed Gardner and Abraham Ribicoff in that key position. Finch did, however, prevail over White House opposition (of the sort that had frustrated his desire to appoint Dr. John Knowles to the top health job) and chose James E. Allen, Jr., as commissioner of education and assistant secretary for education. Allen brought to Washington a distinguished national reputation as New York state's chief education officer. It was said that he had declined John F. Kennedy's offer of the USOE position and in professional education circles his acceptance of the Finch-Nixon bid was seen as a harbinger of hopeful days at 400 Maryland Avenue, S.W.

Constraints on the Commissioner

Commissioner Allen faced many hurdles, however, not least of which was the impotence of his own position. Hundreds of federal programs touched education, but only a fraction of them came under the jurisdiction of the Office of Education. The 1970 budget projected governmentwide outlays for education totalling $9.8 billion (not counting another $1.5 billion to support research and development conducted by universities) of which HEW as a whole would expend 58 percent and the Office of Education only 39 percent.[12] While Allen's domain bulked the largest among the federal fiefdoms involved with education, measured in dollars it contained less than two-fifths of the whole.

Further, a "commissioner," even when he simultaneously wears the label of assistant secretary, does not wield much influence in Washington, particularly when the activities of other agencies are involved. There was little reason for the secretary of defense, the director of the National Science Foundation, or the Veterans Administrator to cede him any authority over their programs, although their agencies accounted for another 22 percent of the total monies. Even within HEW, other units—health, Social Security, and the like—would expend their 19 percent of the federal aggregate without necessarily heeding the policy priorities of the Office of Education.

In 1964 President Johnson had established a Federal Interagency Committee on Education, chaired by the commissioner, to coordinate the education programs of various Washington agencies, but from the outset its power had been minimal. The traditional language appearing in Executive Order 11185—"Nothing in this order shall be construed as subjecting any Federal agency . . . to the authority of any other Federal agency . . ."—effectively barred the committee from any role beyond information gathering and discussion.

That there was no mechanism in the federal establishment for coordinating education programs around unified national policies followed logically enough from the way in which the federal role in American education had evolved. One agency after another might touch on education in the course of discharging its particular mission, but there was no federal education policy as such. There were simply pieces of policies that never came together, save in the annual Budget Bureau tabulation, an exercise more useful for public relations than for policy control.

As early as 1931, a presidential advisory committee had bemoaned the fact that:

The federal government has no inclusive and consistent public policy as to what it should or should not do in the field of education. Whatever particular policies it seems to be pursuing are often inconsistent with each other, sometimes in conflict. They suggest a haphazard development, wherein policies of far-reaching effect have been set up as mere incidents of some special attempt to induce an immediate and particular efficiency.[13]

The situation had not improved when Allen arrived in Washington thirty-eight years later. Indeed the proliferation of programs and agencies in the interim had exacerbated it. The contrast with the new commissioner's home state, where the Board of Regents—and the commissioner on its behalf—enjoys sweeping authority over every aspect of education, could not have been more vivid.

Policy Previews

Two early indications of the Nixon administration's views on education emerged soon after inauguration day, well before Allen even arrived in Washington.

The Republican President needed to declare his intentions with respect to the antipoverty program that was so closely identified with his two Democratic predecessors. So in a Message to Congress on February 19, 1969, Nixon laid out his conception of the proper role of the Office of Economic Opportunity. It was to be predominantly a research and experimentation agency, with its operational programs delegated to the traditional agencies as soon as they had proven themselves. Part of this reorganization entailed shifting the popular Head Start program to HEW. In words crafted primarily by Moynihan, for whom this was the first major presidential policy statement since arriving at the White House, Nixon indicated that despite the disappointing findings of early Head Start evaluations, he remained committed to the program and, more broadly, to the "First Five Years of Life." "Preliminary reports," the president said, "confirm what many have feared: the long term effect of Head Start appears to be extremely weak." Yet seemingly undaunted, he continued, "This must not discourage us," for that weakness was a consequence of the grave educational problems faced by low-income youngsters, not a wholesale failure of the federal program. The message called for redoubled efforts to deal constructively with the environment in which children spent their earliest years, the home as well as formal institutions, and called also for a "national commitment to providing all American children an opportunity for healthful and stimulating development" during their first half decade.[14]

The Moynihan-Nixon language was interesting both for its forthright commitment to a program associated with the Great Society and also for its attempt to employ social science in the determination and explanation of presidential policy. The initial findings of the controversial "Westinghouse Head Start study" were known to Moynihan at the time this message was being prepared, a fact he reminded Nixon of in mid-April when a puzzled president read about the Westinghouse conclusion that Head Start participants showed few gains over equally disadvantaged children who did not take part. That, Moynihan explained, was precisely the point: Head Start was still experimental and should be viewed as part of the administration's larger commitment to test out various approaches to the "first five years."

Just as the learning problems of young children catalyzed the administration's first pronouncement on education, the antics of their older siblings elicited the second. Campus unrest was still spreading, and in mid-March 1969 Secretary Finch wrote the nation's college presidents to remind them that the 90th Congress had required certain forms of federal aid to be denied students whose participation in campus disorders led to criminal convictions.[15] This, it seemed in the White House, provided a fit occasion for the president to state his views on campus unrest. The administration was too new to be charged, as would be common a year later, with actions that precipitated student riots; yet the issue was of crescent national concern and the president could not shun it. A Gallup poll in February had revealed that 82 percent of the public favored the expulsion of students who broke laws in connection with college demonstrations; 84 percent wanted those students' federal loans taken away; and only 25 percent sympathized with the widespread student goal of gaining more say in the running of their colleges.

Against that backdrop, Nixon's March 1969 statement was moderate and restrained. It was another Moynihan product—the urban affairs expert's own Harvard campus would erupt a month later in its nastiest disturbance of many decades—and it staked out a presidential position that was clearly unsympathetic to disruptive students, yet sensitive to some of their complaints and to the fragile nature of the university. "Students today," the president acknowledged, "point to many wrongs which must be made right," including the "depersonalization of the educational experience," the absence of "student involvement in the decision-making process," and the need for new curricula. But the validity of these desires did not justify violence. "The preservation of the integrity, the independence, and the creativity of our institutions of higher learning" concerned Nixon more than the giving or rescinding of individual scholarships and loans. For "civilizations begin to die" when their universities become politicized and violence prone. "The process is altogether too familiar to those who would survey the wreckage of history. Assault and counter assault, one extreme leading to the opposite extreme; the voices of reason and calm discredited."

It was a time, the president said, "to reassert first principles," and he listed two: "That universities and colleges are places of excellence in which men are judged by achievement and merit in defined areas" and "that violence or the threat of violence may never be permitted to influence the actions or judgments of the university community." But no one should look to Washington to police these guidelines, for "the federal government cannot, should not—must not— enforce such principles. That is fundamentally the task and the responsibility of the university community."[16]

No doubt it was tempting to exploit the situation with a sterner antistudent statement. Barely a year later, with the colleges again seething in the aftermath of the Cambodian incursion, the president's unrehearsed crack about the "bums" on campus would reveal what may have been his true feelings from the outset. But it is noteworthy that in the early days of his administration he put his name to a conciliatory statement that clearly left the management of university affairs to the campus community.

Policy Machinery

Promising though they may have been, White House statements on Head Start and campus unrest do not an education policy make, and little movement toward a more comprehensive examination of the subject could be detected in early 1969. Education held no pride of place on the Nixon domestic agenda, and the first half year of his administration witnessed scant attention to this subject at the presidential level.

The principal mechanism in 1969 for identifying domestic issues, elevating them to high level attention, conceptualizing alternatives, and honing specific proposals was the new Council for Urban Affairs, chaired by the president but very much the creature of Executive Secretary Moynihan. That Counselor Burns had his own staff and a mandate to coordinate domestic policy mattered little, for he more often found himself reacting to ideas coming out of the Moynihan office.

The ideas darted about, but the domestic pond was large and held many fish, not all of which could be netted at once. Moynihan had to pick his targets, for due to the council's cumbersome structure—it had a subcommittee for every topic it assayed and plenary sessions to review the reports of the smaller units—and its extravagant demands on the time of cabinet members and their top aides, it was simply not possible to do everything at once. Moynihan's own small staff was mostly new to the ways of the presidency. Its members were so busy with the frequent meetings of the council and its committees that they had little time to cultivate those in the agencies whose daily fare was the policy issues that, in the absence of White House attention, either get resolved or shelved elsewhere in the executive branch.

Topics surfaced in unpredictable ways. A passing comment by the president could give rise to an entire subcommittee, thousands of man-hours of activity, and a full-dress council presentation. Newspaper articles, legislative deadlines, the singular enthusiasms of cabinet members, bright ideas of staff members, outside pressures, books, and magazines—all were sources. Moynihan's own complex sense of what the president was interested in, and of what he wanted the president to be interested in, kept a check on the process and imposed a kind of order. When Nixon flew to Key Biscayne in April 1969, for example, less than three months after his inauguration, he bore a plump notebook, prepared by the Urban Affairs Council staff, containing eight ideas and proposals for immediate action, council consideration, or presidential contemplation.

The central item in the notebook and the heart of the administration's domestic program in the first year was a wholesale reform of the welfare system.

This, energized by the philosophic thrust known as the New Federalism, would culminate in Nixon's television address of August 8 and four accompanying Messages to Congress. Until that day had passed, there was simply not enough energy or time in the domestic portions of the presidency to pay much attention to anything else.

Lack of energy sounds like a weak excuse for slighting topics as large and consequential as education. And, of course, the neglect was not total. Commissioner Allen was busily trying to recruit staff, touching base with his constituency, and surveying his new domain. Others went about their regular tasks as the federal government rounded out a fiscal year (1969) in which it spent nine billion dollars on education and began one in which it would spend almost ten. But in the sense that the presidential government takes a thorough-going look at federal policy in a complex area of domestic activity, rather than presiding over routine management and disposing of occasional issues, education had to wait its turn. Not more than fifteen people in the White House dealt with domestic social policy, and to the extent that one or more of them had to concern himself with a topic before it could be said to be getting presidential attention, many topics lined up in that queue.

From Subcommittee to Working Group

On May 26, 1969, the president established an education subcommittee of the Urban Affairs Council, chaired by HEW Secretary Finch and consisting of Agriculture Secretary Clifford M. Hardin, Attorney General John Mitchell, HUD Secretary George Romney, Labor Secretary George Shultz, OEO Director Rumsfeld, and Budget Bureau Assistant Director Richard P. Nathan. A week later, these men joined Moynihan for an evening cruise on the presidential yacht. Their briefing book for the occasion held background readings on topics ranging from the Coleman Report to the philosophy of liberal education. Its issue papers, prepared by Allen's office, Budget Bureau staffers, and Moynihan aides, posed questions as basic as "Should the level of Federal support for higher education increase, decrease, or remain constant?" and adumbrated problems as distant from federal solution as the "dusty, smelly" condition of urban schools. A proposal to integrate vocational with general education was matched by a journal article on "the economics of inequality."

The boat ride on the Potomac was pleasant and the conversation animated, but education returned to port for another ten weeks as most of the sailors strove to complete the "New Federalism" package. On August 19, however, Moynihan and Finch met in the latter's office and agreed that the time had come for the education subcommittee to start work. The Urban Affairs Council staff promptly began to churn out long agendas of problems and issues ranging from early childhood education to graduate school, although it turned out that the subcommittee did not convene again until early October, and then only for two meetings.

For the entire Urban Affairs Council mechanism was about to stall. In early November the president would overhaul the White House domestic policy apparatus and designate John Ehrlichman as his assistant for domestic affairs, promote Moynihan to the more august but less operational post of counselor, and announce Burns' imminent departure for the Federal Reserve Board. Ehrlichman's deputies assumed control of the policy development process within the Executive Office, including the nascent education message. The Urban Affairs Council, which had been quite successful as a forum for airing issues and a means of equipping a band of high-level Washington newcomers with a perspective on presidential policy making, had proven less suited to forging consensus out of dispute and to transforming ideas into concrete plans. Or so it seemed to the president. By contrast, Ehrlichman and his staff, lawyers rather than scholars or specialists, had shown themselves adept at compromise and detail. Perhaps because he was pleased with Henry Kissinger's success at running a single staff operation in foreign affairs that was able to keep disagreement away from the Oval Office and yet to deliver clear options in usable form, Nixon moved from the overlapping jurisdictions and lively domestic policy debates that marked the early months to a tidier organization chart in which Ehrlichman would parallel Kissinger.

Thus the venue for judging education shifted to a "working group" under the aegis of John Ehrlichman. And it was characteristic of the second phase of domestic policy development in the Nixon White House that the man he assigned to supervise the preparation of the administration's education program was a newcomer to the subject. Edward L. Morgan was a talented young Phoenix lawyer who had served as an advance man during the 1968 campaign and then been asked by Ehrlichman to join the White House legal staff. For some months he worked chiefly on the president's personal legal matters. Then he came to lead the daily meeting at which representatives of various arms of the Executive Office sought to coordinate their legislative strategies. His first total immersion in domestic policy took place when Ehrlichman made him chairman of the working group charged with developing the New Federalism package, where he proved immensely skillful at building a coherent program out of the many shards of policy proposals that a fractious White House staff and cabinet had strewn around the West Wing. In that capacity, he also came into daily contact with the Departments of Labor and HEW and with the Office of Economic Opportunity, and as he got to know those agencies and their key officials, he gradually came to oversee human resource program issues of all kinds and to function as presidential liaison with the principal executive branch units in that field. When Ehrlichman took charge of domestic affairs and set about to divide that large domain into functional areas, it was natural that Morgan should be assigned to the one he was already most familiar with, and there it happened that education topped the agenda.

Amoeba-like, Morgan's working group would split in two by Christmas, as higher education was severed from elementary and secondary. The pair of task forces that followed would actually develop the two Messages to Congress that the president would sign in March 1970. Some men—for reasons I leave to others to explore, there were no women—were habitues of both working groups, while others were chiefly concerned with just one of the messages or a single proposal within it.

Besides Morgan, the White House regulars included Daniel P. Moynihan and this author.

The Bureau of the Budget—later to become the Office of Management and Budget—sent Assistant Director Nathan, the only holdover from the Urban Affairs Council education subcommittee; Emerson J. Elliott, the senior career man in the education (and manpower) area; and Bernard M. Martin, the principal budget examiner for education.

From the Office of Science and Technology came presidential Science Advisor Lee DuBridge, frequently accompanied by his education specialist, John M. Mays.

Herbert Stein represented the Council of Economic Advisors, and the Executive Office contingent was rounded out by OEO representatives Thomas A. Glennan (assistant director) and Donald M. Murdoch (aide to Director Rumsfeld).

Representing the Office of the Secretary of HEW were Assistant Secretary (for Planning and Evaluation) Lewis H. Butler, Deputy Assistant Secretary Robert Patricelli, and a group of their staffers including, from time to time, Martin Kramer, Richard Verville, Michael O'Keefe, Michael Timpane, and Russell Edgerton.

The Office of Education was represented primarily by Commissioner Allen and his executive assistant, Gregory R. Anrig. Deputy Assistant Secretary for Planning, Research and Evaluation James G. Gallagher and Deputy Commissioner Peter Muirhead also participated on occasion.

The Labor Department was the only other cabinet agency with a regular member, Assistant Secretary (for Policy, Evaluation and Research) Jerome Rosow.

The Nature of a Working Group

As a policy-shaping creature, the "working group" enjoyed its greatest prominence in the period between the effective demise of the Urban Affairs Council in the autumn of 1969 and the establishment of the Domestic Council in mid-1970. Both councils consisted of cabinet members heading domestic agencies, plus a scattering of senior officials from various quarters of the Executive Office. But the Ehrlichman working groups were not comprised of cabinet members. Chaired by a staff deputy such as Morgan, each working group was a task force of subcabinet officials drawn from several agencies and from the Executive Office of the President. This simple fact of membership had several significant implications for policy making.

First, the working group was an integral part of a staff rather than a cabinet structure. Headed by a White House aide subordinate to another White House aide who was himself directly answerable to the president, the working group afforded no cabinet member—not even, in the case of education, the secretary of HEW—the automatic right to review, or for that matter even to know about, its policy recommendations. Thus, as Richard P. Nathan has observed, "Direct relationships were established between White House staff and agency officials well below the level of the Secretary. Only the most astute Cabinet member could keep on top of this policy process."[17]

Second, the working group had no constituency except the president. It was not answerable to a congressional committee, as an agency head would be. It could ignore the career officials responsible for running the existing programs in its area of concern. And it could disregard the hopes and fears of the outside interest groups with the greatest stake in the activities under review.

Third, the working group could, and in a sense had to, spend countless hours seeking internal agreement, if not on a single recommendation then at least on a shared perception of the issues and the president's options. While assistant secretaries and White House aides have other demands on their time, their schedules are flexible, their willingness to work late into the night legendary, and their sense of responsibility generally keen. More importantly, the working group is a consensus-seeking creature. Although its membership was largely determined by John Ehrlichman and his deputies—who could and did reach into the executive agencies for participants without necessarily asking the department head to designate his choices—and although the membership was fluid enough that individuals could be added or subtracted at any point in the process, the typical working group had as its principal task the preparation of a "decision paper" for the president. Because there was no intervening level, no cabinet committee to argue the merits of various ideas in front of the president as the Urban Affairs Council had done, the decision paper was both a brief and a form of final judgment on an issue. Operating within such a format, the working group could not fulfill its responsibilities simply by giving the president the classic "three options"—do nothing, do something, do a great deal—with four demurrers and two exceptions for each alternative and a minority report arguing that the issue had been poorly framed. Such a report would simply put the burden back on the president without providing the guidance the working group mechanism was intended to supply. But neither was a working group a representative body which made decisions by voting on choices. Democratic procedure is ill suited to reconciling the Budget Bureau's concern over expenditure levels, the Office of Education's ardor for new programs, the science advisor's perception of the technological consequences of a course of action, and the antipoverty agency's estimate of its impact on the poor and disadvantaged.

Moreover, the Ehrlichman staff did not consist of subject matter specialists who might resolve intragroup disputes on the basis of their own expertise. They were typically lawyers like Morgan, trained to weigh evidence and compromise differences, personally detached from the substance of matters they were given charge of, and reluctant to rely on their own knowledge or their ex officio power to impose a conclusion on a group of other persons who also had presidential commissions on their walls and several of whom had at least the latent ability to go back to their agency heads and advise them that the views and interests of their departments were being disregarded by a White House functionary.

As John Ehrlichman added to his personal power over the months and years, as he and his deputies grew more confident that their views would prevail with the president, and as cabinet members and agency officials became ever more subordinated to the swelling White House staff, much of this lawyerly disinterestedness and personal diffidence would erode. But in 1969 and 1970, when the working group mode was new, when the professorial presence at the White House of experts such as Moynihan and Burns was consequential, and when many could still recall Richard Nixon's pledge to run an "open presidency," policy options and recommendations flowing into the Oval Office were expected—by Ehrlichman, at least, by H.R. Haldeman, the final arbiter of what the president would see, and very likely by Nixon himself—to reflect something close to an administration-wide consensus on a substantive matter.

Largely by accident of timing, education came to the fore during this period when the Urban Affairs Council was decaying, when the Ehrlichman staff was still new to its domestic policy responsibilities, when—within limits—"experts" were accorded a measure of respect at the White House and their views taken seriously, and when the Domestic Council was as yet nothing more than an idea buried in the private deliberations of the President's Advisory Council on Executive Organization.

It happened, again mostly by chance, that many of the members of the education panels were also veterans of the prototype working group that had shaped the president's welfare reform and "New Federalism" proposals during the previous spring and summer. Morgan, Moynihan, Nathan, Butler, Patricelli, and Rosow were accustomed to working together, respected one another, and enjoyed an easy camaraderie. For them, the education working groups were a natural, and less taxing, revival of a hit show. That none of them, with the partial exception of Moynihan, was an "educationist" concerned them very little. (Allen and DuBridge, the "newcomers," were of course both educators.) None of them had been a social worker either, but the president had accepted their previous work, and the proposals based on it had been widely acclaimed as the most promising domestic initiatives of the Nixon presidency.

None of these men was an ideologue. Apart from Moynihan, most were avowed Republicans, but with the likely exception of Morgan they would have described themselves as liberal or moderate Republicans and as not being the least hostile to federal activity in a domestic field such as education provided that activity were well-conceived, well-executed, and not inordinately expensive. They would approach questions of federal education policy much as they had the tangled strands of welfare policy: a bit skeptical of the Great Society programs, confident that a better definition of the federal role awaited articulation, doubtful that specialists in the field possessed the wisdom necessary for that better definition, certain that Richard Nixon would take their considered views seriously, and fairly sanguine that the nation—if not the specialists, the interest groups, or perhaps even the Congress—would respond favorably to well-founded presidential initiatives.

Elementary and Secondary Education

When the Urban Affairs Council subcommittee on education finally assembled on October 3, 1969, less than two weeks remained before Finch and Allen were scheduled to explain to a Senate Appropriations Subcommittee why the administration did not want the billion extra dollars that the House had added to the Office of Education budget. Nixon had already indicated that even if it were appropriated he had no intention of spending it, which thus left the secretary and his commissioner the thankless task of trying to talk the traditionally liberal and education-minded Senate out of following the lower chamber's lead without making the administration appear needlessly unsympathetic to school teachers and students.

In a strategy session at HEW a few days before the subcommittee meeting, Finch, Moynihan, Allen, and their aides concluded that one escape from this awkward dilemma was to move fast enough that the full Urban Affairs Council could review an education program in time for the president to announce it prior to the appropriation hearing. The administration would thus have something affirmative to propose in the realm of education before stating its reasons why additional money should not be pumped into existing programs.

This was a large order. The next council meeting was scheduled for October tenth. The Senate hearing was slated for the fourteenth, and if a credible package of policies and programs were to be ready by that date the long-dormant subcommittee would have time for two meetings at most.

Moynihan confidently said it could be done, and Finch and Allen, willing to try anything, were eager to make the attempt. It would turn out to be five months before the message emerged that was initially planned to take but two weeks. Yet in those hectic days and nights of early October it did look for a while as though the earlier deadline might be met.

Although the subcommittee had not gathered since its June dinner cruise, a good deal of staff-level thinking had gone on in the interim. I had worked up a long memorandum that set out a dozen topics for consideration, ranging from the fiscal travails of parochial schools to the problem of campus unrest. None was a program as such, but rather an area or issue on which the subcommittee might focus. The fiscal 1971 budget season was also getting under way, and the BOB examiners had written a series of papers reviewing some of the key education policy issues. Members of Finch's staff at HEW had also developed a set of options for the secretary. And Commissioner Allen, who had just announced the "Right to Read" as the nation's top education priority for the years ahead, had some additional thoughts of his own.

In the planning meeting at Finch's office, the secretary indicated that his own compelling interests in education, aside from the urgent tactical need to get the administration publicly committed to something constructive prior to that vexing session on Capitol Hill, were community colleges and black colleges. Moynihan talked about the Coleman Report, the disappointing record of the big compensatory education programs, and his keen desire to make educational research and development more scientific. As the government's chief education spokesman, Allen was particularly worried about the administration's seeming apathy to the desires of his constituency, so he dwelt on the need to take a more forthcoming stance and stated his eagerness to turn the Right to Read from a slogan into a program. The knotty subject of school finance also came up, as Finch recalled that the creation of some sort of commission on educational finance had interested the president in earlier conversations.

At the meeting's end, Bob Patricelli, Tim Wirth (then a deputy assistant secretary of HEW for education, later to become a Democratic congressman from Colorado), and I were assigned to turn this ragout of ideas and concerns into a report that the Urban Affairs Council could review less than two weeks later.

The next morning, we three huddled with Richard Verville and Michael O'Keefe of Patricelli's staff. After arranging for Finch's secretary to call a meeting of the education subcommittee for October third, we parcelled out the tasks to be completed for that review. Obeying what we understood to be the guidelines emerging from the previous day's strategy session, we determined that the subcommittee should first take up the matter of compensatory education, which also seemed like a sensible way to bring its members into some basic understanding of the general stance we hoped the administration would take. Reflecting Finch's and Moynihan's predilections, we intended to steer the subcommittee, most of whose other members had scant familiarity with these issues, toward a policy for elementary and secondary education that would stress research and experimentation, with particular reference to disadvantaged youngsters and their compensatory needs. Recent evaluations of Head Start and Title I (of the Elementary and Secondary Education Act) had found a worrisome lack of impact by these two large Great Society programs and lent force to the notion that easing the educational distress of poor youngsters would require a much more sophisticated research strategy. One promising initiative that we wished to highlight was the Experimental Schools Program, which had been budgeted at $25 million but for which the House had voted no money, even while adding the extra billion to other education programs. We expected that these ideas, together with a review of the structure of educational finance, would fill the subcommittee's agenda at its first session and, we hoped, would also dominate the report and proposals we intended to have ready for a second meeting soon thereafter.

Our small staff group, together with Dr. James Gallagher, USOE's top research official, met almost continuously for three days to work out the subcommittee presentation, prepare "talking points" for Finch and Allen, and ready charts and other materials.

All the members showed up on October third, save for the secretary of agriculture and the attorney general. The meeting went smoothly, with Finch, Allen, Moynihan, and Gallagher each making a presentation and the other cabinet officers listening attentively and asking thoughtful questions. Only the chart-and-slide presentation on compensatory education seemed weak and therein lay the seeds of a persistent dispute between the Office of Education and the rest of the administration.

Whereas Moynihan, Finch, and their aides were prepared to postulate the failure of existing compensatory education programs and proceed from there, Allen, Gallagher, and their colleagues were understandably reluctant to assert that these programs to which they were so deeply committed had not succeeded or at least that they could not succeed if funded more amply.

Thus Finch began the meeting by announcing his conclusion that the extant programs were not working well and that he was wary of applying more money to them until the theories on which they were based had been better tested and refined. Moynihan followed with an eloquent rendition of the findings and policy implications of the Coleman Report, coming to the same conclusions as Finch. But when Gallagher's turn came, though he did not contradict his department head or the presidential aide, he let it be known that he was less than wholly persuaded by available evidence that the shortcomings of existing compensatory programs might not be fixed by an infusion of additional resources.

This disagreement remained beneath the surface at the October third meeting, but not far. In fact, the available data were ambiguous and could be interpreted to support a number of conclusions. The Coleman Report had said little about federal compensatory schemes *per se,* and the assessments of Title I and Head Start were susceptible to the charge that the programs, being new, unevenly administered and modestly funded, were not ready for final judgments, especially when the evaluation studies themselves had some methodological problems.

Moynihan and Finch held firmly to the view that these studies amply documented the need for more basic research into the learning process itself, that to continue to boost existing programs as solutions to the educational problems of the disadvantaged was dishonest as well as costly, and that the responsible course of action for the administration was to let the popular programs endure but also to stress their shortcomings and uncertainties so as to create a climate in which the nation would be receptive to the needed research and experimentation.

Having recently taken the helm of OE's research and development program, Gallagher was certainly not hostile to added research, but was cautious about using limited and possibly flawed results of available studies as the basis for debunking the ongoing compensatory programs. For his part, Allen held a reasoned and deep-seated commitment to reform of the nation's schools and was willing to point to their weaknesses in order to generate enthusiasm for buttressing them. But he feared that the administration he had lately joined was well on its way to developing an anti-education stance, he found the tendency to oppose spending additional dollars on schooling most distasteful, and he wanted to exercise great care in any criticism of the educational process that might emanate from HEW or the White House.

The subcommittee meeting closed with a mandate to the staff to prepare a report for another session five days later. The goal was still to have such a report approved by the subcommittee on October eighth for submission to the full Urban Affairs Council on the tenth.

Two related events occurred in the first few days of October. The Budget Bureau education staff held a general review session with Nathan to discuss priorities for the 1971 budget and found itself in broad agreement with the ideas then beginning to germinate in the Urban Affairs Council. Characterized as the "four -ations," the concepts of demonstration, experimentation, evaluation, and dissemination struck the career budget examiners and Nathan as reasonable areas for emphasis for the coming year's spending plans.

During the discussions leading up to the first subcommittee meeting, one staff member recalled that a year earlier candidate Nixon had proposed something called a National Institute for the Educational Future. A hasty check of the campaign speeches proved that he had indeed outlined a new federal unit that could readily be transformed into a structural basis for the administration's mounting interest in better educational research.

It appeared that the White House, the Budget Bureau, and the Office of the Secretary of HEW, moving toward a common, if still vague, policy position for elementary and secondary education, had chanced upon a vehicle that might carry the administration in the direction they wanted it to take. That the Office of Education did not fully share their conclusions mattered little.

Dick Verville and I spent a frantic weekend drafting the subcommittee report. By the time we finished, it had grown to a thirty-page document giving a history of federal education programs, a description of the compensatory programs, a summary of their recent evaluations, a discussion of the policy implications of the Coleman Report, a sketch of the school finance issue and a series of recommendations, including a commission to study educational finance and the new national institute that the president had proposed.

The report bulked too large, so while it was being revised and typed on Monday and Tuesday, the staff decided to prepare a shorter version as well. This was written largely by Lewis Butler, who had emerged in the preceding week as *de facto* chairman of our group.

He and I grabbed the summary and walked down the hall late Tuesday to brief Finch and to fix the agenda for the following day's subcommittee meeting, which the secretary would again chair. He concurred with all the staff recommendations, then added that he would also like to see some discussion of community colleges. This subject was still on his mind, and he indicated that the department was under pressure from Congress to do something for these burgeoning institutions.

Meanwhile bad news arrived in the form of a message from the president's appointments secretary that the meeting of the full Urban Affairs Council had been postponed from October tenth to the seventeenth. This obviously threw off the whole schedule, since the goal had been to issue a presidential statement on education before the Senate hearing on the fourteenth.

Butler met at the White House with John Ehrlichman, and they decided that Finch should see the president on Friday, the tenth, even though there was no council meeting. Perhaps some sort of statement could still be produced in time.

The subcommittee met on Wednesday, as planned—at least part of it did. At the last moment, the president summoned Moynihan. Labor Secretary Shultz could not attend either. Far too many HEW staffers showed up, and despite his detailed briefing on the contents of the draft report, Finch insisted on devoting most of the discussion to community colleges, which had nothing to do with the document the group was supposed to review.

The meeting went terribly, and Attorney General Mitchell, who sat puffing on his pipe and glowering throughout, remarked to an aide as he walked out of HEW that the snow would fly before he would be found back in that building. As the staff sat glumly in Butler's office after the session, wondering what to do next, it was clear that the subcommittee had failed to take any action it could report to the full Urban Affairs Council and was unlikely to meet again soon.

Two days later, however, Finch had his meeting with the president. He and Moynihan, who joined him in the Oval Office, took advantage of a delay in Nixon's schedule to write out a hasty memorandum urging that the president send Congress a message on education within the next two weeks. They suggested six points for such a message: the national research institute and school finance commission already in the draft report; a new program to aid community colleges; a request that Congress restore the funds for experimental schools; an inquiry by HEW into the problems of black colleges; and an increase in GI Bill education benefits for Vietnam veterans.

Nixon liked these ideas and gave his approval in principle to the concept of an education message and to the six proposals as probable elements of it. He then handed the Finch-Moynihan memorandum to John Ehrlichman and instructed him to work it into a detailed set of program specifications. That simple action had the effect of taking jurisdiction away from the Urban Affairs Council structure and bestowing it on Ehrlichman's staff, which a few weeks later was formally to be given responsibility for all domestic policy matters.

For the time being, however, the Urban Affairs Council was still a going concern, and while entrusting Ehrlichman with the preparation of the Message to Congress, the president also approved the items in the Finch-Moynihan list as the agenda for the following week's council meeting. In the interim, Finch and Allen would have to absorb any heat from the Appropriations Committee themselves.

Thus the once-urgent deadline of the Senate hearing passed, and education policy was now to be addressed in its own right, first through discussion in the Cabinet room and then by a working group that Ehrlichman would form to prepare concrete proposals for the president.

The council meeting was animated and evidenced general agreement that a message on education was a good idea and that the national education institute and a commission to study school finance were worthy entries in it. Commissioner Allen also roused some cabinet-level enthusiasm for his Right to Read idea, and the president seemed generally pleased. It may be noted, however, that this session in mid-October was the last time a group of cabinet members discussed education prior to the messages the following March, save for the issue of school desegregation, which would soon have a cabinet committee of its own.

Drafts and Redrafts

Under Morgan's leadership, the education working group started fast. Six days after the Urban Affairs Council discussed it, a draft Message to Congress was being circulated. Significantly, this initial version came out of Butler's office at HEW, not from the Office of Education, although Allen and his executive assistant, Gregory Anrig, where charter members of the working group that reviewed it.

A second draft—mine—followed on October twenty-fourth. Each was circulated for comment to the working group members, and for a time it looked as though a developing consensus would permit the package to go to the president quite rapidly.

But then, as so often happens when many people are involved and when they have no firm deadline to work against, doubts began to get voiced and major changes suggested.

The Bureau of the Budget concluded that there should be no education message in the autumn. The president's annual State of the Union Message was little more than two months away, and Budget Director Robert Mayo urged Moynihan to take the two principal education proposals—the institute and the commission—and have the president announce them in that format. The Bureau's fear, shared by Rumsfeld and Glennan at OEO, was that any low-budget presidential program in the field of education would look like a weak substitute for the extra money that Congress was seeking to spend on schools and colleges and that since the administration would not commit the funds necessary to retrieve the initiative, it was better not to draw attention to the subject at all.

Demurrers also arrived from Allen, who found the tone of the draft message unduly critical of the nation's education system and the hard-working professionals who staffed it. He also fretted that the administration's obstinate refusal to commit more funds to education, and the message's justification of that stance, were both wrong in themselves and certain to receive a frigid response from the education community and the Congress. But the commissioner expressed himself poorly, articulated his doubts weakly, and generally failed to persuade other members of the Morgan group that his concerns warranted theirs.

Meanwhile, Moynihan tried with markedly greater success to impress upon his working group colleagues that the substantive proposals and the dollars behind them mattered less than the analysis embedded in the draft message. He argued that the historic importance of this presidential statement lay in its assertion by the chief executive of a post-Coleman criterion for education itself. The preeminent finding of the past decade's social research in the field of education, Moynihan held, was how little student achievement seemed to vary with the type of school attended and how modest were the differential effects of alterations in such familiar school inputs as expenditure, class size, and teacher training. Pupil achievement varied enormously, to be sure—Coleman's data on this were overwhelming and it was apparent to the casual observer as well—but the principal correlates and presumed sources of that variation lay in forces such as home and peer group that the schools had little control over.

This reasoning led to the conclusion that pumping additional funds into some schools so that they could afford to become more like other schools was unlikely to have significant effect on how much their students learned. Hence playing along with the conventional wisdom that it would was a cruel deception, particularly for the disadvantaged youngsters of the nation. The state of the art of educational research was as yet too primitive to permit any proposals for intervention, whether in schools or in students' environment, that could confidently be said to insure heightened achievement. This should be stated boldly, Moynihan argued, and accompanied by a proposal for more and better research. Finally, the president should jolt the public and the education community by asserting an obvious yet ill-recognized basis for judging the entire educational enterprise: What matters is not how much money is spent on schools but how much their students learn.

That conclusion was scarcely likely to win much support from educators, particularly when voiced by a president reluctant to spend more on schools. Nor were output measures in the form of achievement test scores very satisfactory to men and women convinced that equally important gauges of educational success were such hard-to-quantify accomplishments as socialization, emotional growth, and esthetic development. To argue that the vast national education enterprise should, in effect, be denied the resources that professional schoolmen insisted they needed to carry out its many responsibilities to society until some unknown future time when researchers should have succeeded in plumbing the unknowns of cognition was unquestionably a bold approach, but not one that

Allen, Gallagher, and others from the Office of Education were eager to have espoused by the president they served.

But this seemingly fundamental debate soon became one of tone and rhetoric rather than substance. No one in the working group believed that large additional federal resources for education were anywhere to be found in the near term, much as some members would have wished it otherwise. At no time did a draft of the message contain any costly new initiatives or any promise of a greatly expanded federal role in the financing of education. At one point, the debate between White House message drafters and USOE executives actually came down to a single adverb: whether the president should say that the prospect of larger appropriations would be pursued "simultaneously" with more intensive research into the learning process or deferred until that research had born fruit. The final version fudged the distinction by saying "As we get more education for the dollar, we will ask the Congress to supply many more dollars for education."

October gave way to November, and a decision was made to hold back the education message until the president had outlined his overall domestic philosophy in January's State of the Union Message. That annual address had traditionally opened the season of special messages fleshing out the details of administration proposals in particular policy arenas, and the Nixon White House elected to follow that pattern.

Throughout the late autumn of 1969, draft after draft of the education message continued to move around by White House messenger to members of the working group. The unresolved matter of the "extra billion" remained a troublesome backdrop. But except for a decision to deal separately with higher education issues and their consequent elimination from what White House staffers occasionally referred to as the "lower education" message, the content of the administration program changed very little between October and March.

The National Institute of Education

The centerpiece of the president's message became the proposal to create a new National Institute of Education—modeled in part on the venerable and respected National Institutes of Health—to conduct research into all aspects of education.[1]

It was not a novel idea. In 1958, an education panel organized by the National Academy of Sciences had suggested the creation of such an agency. Six years later, a unit of the President's Science Advisory Committee picked up the notion. In 1969, it reappeared in David Krathwohl's presidential address to the American Educational Research Association, and a year after that it showed up as one of the central recommendations of the Commission on Instructional Technology, which was chaired by Sterling McMurrin, one of Allen's predecessors as U.S. commissioner of education.[2]

Although it is uncertain whether the campaign speechwriter who put the idea of a National Institute for the Educational Future into candidate Nixon's mouth in 1968 was familiar with these precedents, it is clear that when HEW and White House aides seized upon the notion in the autumn of 1969, it was the campaign address rather than the earlier versions that was in their minds. In fact, the McMurrin commission report was to prove something of an embarrassment, since its release prior to the president's message would "steal his thunder" (a problem which was solved by simply withholding the report from public view for a time).

But the institute was not proposed *because* Nixon had suggested it during his campaign, although that recollection proved helpful in marketing the idea within the administration. It was proposed because it appeared to serve several utilitarian purposes.

Once the Moynihan-Coleman logic was embraced, and with it the proposition that more and better educational research was needed, the question naturally arose how best might such research be managed within the federal establishment.

No one in the working group was pleased with the performance of USOE's Bureau of Research, recently renamed the National Center for Educational Research and Development. In one stormy review session, Moynihan, Nathan, and Morgan had pressed Gallagher to cite a single instance of research conducted under its auspices that had produced useful or significant results, and they had been wholly unsatisfied with the stumbling response. The Budget Bureau faulted NCERD for planning badly, wasting money, and exercising weak direction of its projects. The education specialists on Butler's staff concurred, as did DuBridge's aides and the President's Science Advisory Committee. Federal educational research funds were scant, were heavily committed to the support of a network of regional laboratories and university research centers, and were largely in the hands of traditional educational researchers, a group whose disciplinary breadth and intellectual distinction did not impress those members of the working group who knew something of social science and of scholarship.

Broadening the definition of educational research, enlarging and deepening the pool of scientific talent that it could be immersed in, and cutting loose from the ineffectual bureau that managed it all seemed essential. Historically, such considerations have often given rise to a new agency—a move that may also help to meet some of a president's political and public relations needs—for in the absence of glossy new programs and hefty outlays, it is not unheard of to propose a revised structure.

The working group never seriously considered placing the new agency outside the Department of Health, Education and Welfare. The idea was simply to distinguish it from the Office of Education. The fact that the commissioner of education also happened to be the assistant secretary for education suggested an obvious arrangement and forestalled any opposition from Allen: Place the new agency under the assistant secretary, but not within USOE.

The next question was what to do with the extant research authority of the Office of Education. Working group members felt that most present efforts in this field were so weak that they would rapidly be eclipsed by those of the new institute and agreed that ultimately any worth preserving should be transferred into the fledgling agency. Its older counterpart would then no longer need to engage in educational research at all. Even Gallagher, who may have hoped he would emerge as a likely candidate to direct the institute, hailed this decision since he had argued persuasively that it was ludicrous to have two parallel and overlapping research agencies. Of course, the amalgamation also meant that the Office of Education's research budget could be included in the totals projected for the institute, which permitted the president to announce a respectable sum—"when fully developed . . . as much as a quarter of a billion dollars"— without causing undue anxiety in the Budget Bureau.

The structure and responsibilities of the new agency—which the working group called the National Learning Institute until Gallagher and Allen persuaded their colleagues that in professional circles "learning" was too narrowly construed—drew forth volumes of memoranda at the staff level and provided the meat for thousands of hours of earnest discussion. The gestation of a new federal agency is an exciting time, an event that seldom occurs more than once during a typical Washington aide's tour of duty and therefore one worth savoring.

Most of the operational decisions got made outside the working group, although periodically staffers would clear them with their principals. The institute was to have a broad and flexible mandate, the ability—like NIH, but unlike the Office of Education—to conduct some intramural research, and the authority to go outside civil service regulations to hire talented scholars for its professional staff. In time, though not before the president's message, HEW would contract with Roger E. Levien of the RAND Corporation to do a detailed planning study.[3] But the bill that went to Congress hard on the heels of the president's message was primarily the work of Butler's staff, the Budget Bureau, and myself, with drafting assistance from HEW lawyers. USOE officials had little to do with this process, although Allen and Gallagher periodically reacted to working papers. The career staff of NCERD—the unit that was to be replaced— was all but frozen out of the process.

Little effort was made to consult anyone outside the executive branch either. The administration was generally close-mouthed, the working group confident, and the staff busy. Moynihan and I periodically solicited advice from Coleman and from Dean Theodore Sizer and other former colleagues and friends at the Harvard Graduate School of Education. The education panel of the President's Science Advisory Committee held a lively discussion of the institute idea in December, and I accompanied Gallagher to an informative session at Stanford in mid-winter, but few other efforts were made to garner advice and opinions or to build support for the institute idea among the organizations and interest groups that would be its logical constituency.

This failure was part of a larger problem: The working group simply kept what it was doing to itself. Preoccupied with the need to resolve differences among its own members, the process of consensus building never moved beyond the executive branch. Congressmen and their aides were not consulted. Journalists were not briefed (until the day of the message) other than through a few intentional leaks. Education lobbyists were ignored.

Such an inward-looking policy process was characteristic of the early Nixon administration. Good ideas there were, but until the day they were announced to the world they were secrets confined to the political appointees of the executive branch and such career officials as needed to know. Once the president signed his name to the proposals, an ambitious and sometimes quite sophisticated public relations process would begin, but by not even giving key interest groups the courtesy of advance consultation, all later attempts at building support had to reckon with a higher level of suspicion than perhaps needed to be the case.

In the case of the national institute, two added conditions worked against any advance rallying of interest groups. Because the "extra billion dollars" loomed above the entire sequence, there seemed little to be gained from trying to convince the major professional organizations—the National Education Association, the Council of Chief State School Officers, and the like—of the merits of a low budget package that not only refused to spend large additional sums of federal money but that twisted the knife by lecturing the education establishment on its habit of letting input measures substitute for outcomes.

As for educational researchers, perhaps the group most likely to respond to a skillful advance pitch for the institute idea, they were part of the problem that the proposal was intended to solve: the historic domination of educational research by a fraternity of scholars inhabiting teachers colleges and education schools and the corresponding tendency of topflight social scientists to eschew the subject. Why then go to the American Educational Research Association in search of endorsements? If the institute evolved as the working group hoped, not many AERA members would wind up spending its money.

As finally proposed, the National Institute of Education had some additional features whose presence in the presidential message attests to the *modus operandi* and membership of the working group.

The Right to Read

This was Commissioner Allen's special enthusiasm. He had announced it in September 1969 as a fundamental goal for the nation; "education's moonshot for the Seventies" he sometimes said. His central notion was both simple and laudable: Too many Americans were functionally illiterate and, regardless of their age, Allen felt that helping them learn to read was an obvious and important mission that was well-suited to federal leadership.

Unfortunately, the commissioner had no clear-cut program tailored to this objective. Asserting a national goal is one thing, but figuring out how to get there is something else, and how Allen intended to try never came through very clearly to those in HEW, the Budget Bureau, and the White House who had to reckon with his insistence that the administration embrace the goal. On the other hand, it was patently not a bad idea that everyone should know how to read, and the president had personally shown some interest when Allen described his idea at the October meeting of the Urban Affairs Council. The absence of a specific program meant no pressure on the budget, although it posed something of a credibility program in associating the president with a goal that lacked visible means of attainment.

In trying to look credible, the message ended up a bit deceptive, a victim of the old budget shell game: Take some money already budgeted for existing programs—in this case, Titles II and III of the Elementary and Secondary Education Act—and announce that it will be spent in furtherance of some new purpose not obviously embraced by the ongoing activities. Of the $200 million that the president announced he would ask Congress to appropriate for these programs in the context of the Right to Read, all but $35 million was already in the budget for the accustomed purposes: the purchase of school library books and the support of state-planned supplementary centers and services. Although the activities underwritten by these funds were not unrelated to the Right to Read and could doubtless be made more useful to it, the money was allocated in ways that left the initiative to state and local authorities. Hence enlarging these programs did not give the Office of Education a penny exclusively for the Right to Read nor did it give the commissioner any leverage for putting his ill-defined plans into practice.

A further complication cropped up in the form of parochial schools. For months, Nixon had been pressing his aides to figure out some Constitutional means of assisting the Catholic schools, then in the midst of a well-publicized fiscal crisis. When he met with a group of Catholic educators in late February 1970, they told him that the existing program from which their schools derived the greatest benefit was Title II, the books-for-school-libraries authority. The president said he would see that they got more, and Charles W. Colson, whose White House function at the time was liaison with special interest groups, emerged from that meeting determined to see Title II increased by $200 million.[4]

There ensued a classic example of the staff scurrying to redefine the president's short-run instructions in order to accord better with its view of his long-range interests and priorities. The Budget Bureau was scandalized at the thought of adding such a large sum to the fiscal 1971 budget. Colson insisted that money be found to keep the president's pledge to the Catholic educators. Allen wanted some flexible funds for the Right to Read. And the rest of the working group, not very avid about either Allen's notion or Colson's commitment, chose to satisfy these incompatible needs by lumping Titles II and III together, upping the total to $200 million, wrapping the banner of the Right to Read around it, and rhetorically lodging the whole package under the National Institute of Education although the programs were conducted by *USOE*.

Television and Learning

One of the foremost notions in the 1968 campaign proposal of a National Institute for the Educational Future had been the application of modern technology to the learning process. Television would naturally rank near the top of any listing of technological developments that bear on education. It happened that this linkage was a particular passion of speechwriter William Safire, who was assigned to translate the working group's proposals into the language of a presidential message. It also happened that the legislation authorizing the Corporation for Public Broadcasting was expiring, and that a separate White House task force had just finished designing a new approach to financing the CPB. That bill was ready to go to Congress, and the education message seemed like as good a way as any for the president to announce it, particularly since HEW staffers had been struggling for months to devise a suitable federal position on the educational uses of television.

All of this had little to do with the National Institute of Education as it was emerging with a strong slant toward basic research, and the Corporation for Public Broadcasting had even less relevance. But there was to be a message on education which needed whatever substantive proposals it could get, and educational television was not entirely unrelated. So in went a few paragraphs on the subject, although Morgan and Safire successfully foiled my repeated attempts to insert an endorsement of "Sesame Street," which failed of inclusion ostensibly on the grounds of taste. (Presidents, I was told, do not plug individual television shows, no matter how meritorious.)

Experimental Schools

This subject got only one brief paragraph: a renewed appeal to Congress to restore the $25 million that the administration had earlier requested for the new Experimental Schools program and that had been deleted by the House of Representatives. In addition to thinking Experimental Schools a good idea in its own right and one that was compatible with the principal thrust of the message, the working group welcomed the chance to chide Congress for spending too little on at least one area of education.

The President's Commission on School Finance

In September 1969, Secretary Finch had observed that the president was personally interested in creating a commission to look into the manifold intricacies of educational finance.

The topic had drawn much public attention. Several recent books, including Arthur Wise's *Rich Schools, Poor Schools*, had documented the disparities that reliance on local property taxes and state funding formulae creates in the resources available to public schools in neighboring communities.[5] The first of many law suits had been filed to test the Constitutionality of such discrepancies. How, the plaintiffs asked, could a state claim to provide equal protection of the laws when the schools of a prosperous town might spend twice or thrice the amount per student as those in a poverty-stricken jurisdiction, even though they levied the same tax rates and benefited from the same state aid program?

The rejection by local taxpayers of school bond issues was also much in the news, as was the special fiscal plight of nonpublic schools across the land. Urban schools were another problem; quite aside from the doubtful efficacy of compensatory programs was the simple fact that big cities had so many other demands on their tax resources that some could ill afford the money to maintain even minimum standards of adequacy in their deteriorating educational institutions.

The time was right, or so it seemed, for a thoroughgoing look at this whole subject. The State of Michigan had recently completed such an examination, and administration aides were much impressed by Governor Milliken's proposal for the state to assume the entire burden of school finance. Perhaps the president could appoint a distinguished group to scrutinize the issue and develop some sensible recommendations for the nation.

Lurking in the background was the administration's political problem posed by Congress'—and the education lobbyists'—insistence that Washington supply a larger share of the nation's school budget. One way to defer, if not to deflect, this nettlesome challenge was through the familiar route of designating a group to study it.[6]

The Urban Affairs Council education subcommittee had discussed the notion of a school finance commission in October; the president had approved the idea at his private session with Finch and Moynihan; and it was again reviewed by the full Urban Affairs Council on October seventeenth. The working group never doubted that it was to be one of the pieces of the administration's education package. The only questions were how to establish it, what mandate to give it, and what to say about it.

The message was expansive on this subject. The commission would puzzle out the entire tax structure and funding practices that states and localities employed in the course of channelling money to their schools. Over its two-year lifespan it was to report "to the President periodically on future revenue needs and fiscal priorities," and it was "to study the different approaches being pioneered by States and local districts, and to disseminate the information about successes achieved and problems encountered at the local level."a

The working group entertained the idea of asking Congress to create the commission by statute, but at Butler's urging settled on an executive order instead. It fell to me, with the help of technical experts in the Budget Bureau, to draft the order.

This section of the message became the locus of three further concerns. The administration's revenue-sharing proposals would, if enacted, channel considerable additional funds to the states and localities, and it was noteworthy that such resources could be used for education which, the message observed, typically consumed two-fifths of state and local revenues. Revenue sharing, and the further savings that would accrue to states from the administration's proposed welfare reforms, were not obviously aimed at the finance of schools, but they could well have that effect and it was worth saying so.

The old program of aid to "federally-impacted areas," on the other hand, exemplified a contradictory thrust. That popular scheme, which the administration had recently proposed to curtail, "neither assists States to determine their own education expenditures," the message asserted, "nor re-directs funds to the individual districts in greatest need." If federal monies were going to go into education, the working group felt, this was a model of how not to do it, and the president should say that, too.

Nonpublic schools also reappeared in this section of the message. They had financial troubles, too, and the frequent reports of parochial school closings suggested that perhaps their woes were even graver than those of their public sector counterparts. The president's meeting with the Catholic educators had also resulted in a pledge to set up a panel of some sort to study—and in so doing to highlight—their fiscal difficulties, and Charles Colson dashed off to create one.

This was another instance of the staff's left hand not being well connected to the right, for—partly because Moynihan and Morgan were both out of town at the time—no one from the education working group attended that meeting and no one who was present knew much about what the education working group was considering.

It was patently absurd to create two separate commissions on school finance, particularly when the interplay of public and private schools surely had something to do with the fiscal condition of each. Moreover, there had recently been a lot of publicity about private "segregation academies" being opened in southern communities by persons seeking to spare their children from public school integration, and sudden White House attention to nonpublic schools could be construed as presidential endorsement of this evasion. This was not

aThe full text of Richard M. Nixon's "Special Message to the Congress on Education Reform," March 3, 1970, appears in Appendix A of this volume. Throughout this chapter, all presidential quotations are taken from this message unless otherwise indicated.

anyone's intent—Nixon was genuinely, if for obvious political reasons, desirous of appearing sympathetic to the problems of Catholic schools—and eventually the two commission ideas were merged. The message ended up with a vigorous endorsement of the "diversity" afforded the nation by having public and private schools operating alongside one another, and the executive order awkwardly stipulated that the President's Commission on School Finance would have a separate "panel" on nonpublic schools. But the Oval Office pledge to the Catholic educators was honored, too, for Nixon separately announced the "panel" when he named its four members on April 21, two months before appointing the other commissioners.

Early Learning

As it emerged in the President's education message of March 1970, the "Early Learning Program" was a fraud. Billed as a joint undertaking by HEW and OEO "to establish a network of experimental centers to discover what works best in early childhood education," it was nothing more nor less than a restatement of the administration's previous—and largely unfulfilled—commitment to "the First Five Years of Life." It was, as the speechwriters say, a throwaway, and everyone on the working group knew that. Why it remained in the final message, a document that otherwise boasted some textual integrity, says more about what happens when writers take part in substantive deliberations than anything else. Safire liked the idea—it allowed him to use a nice quip about "child's play" being "serious business"—and he insisted on it. Weary from months of haggling over the substance and phrasing of the message, the other members of the working group let it go and consoled themselves with the thought that it at least increased by one the number of entries in an otherwise slender program package.

The President's Involvement

Although Richard Nixon did not sit down with a yellow pad and write his education message, he made the acquaintance of its principal elements early in the drafting process, and was kept reasonably well informed as it progressed. On October tenth, he had approved the idea of a Message to Congress on this subject and had provisionally okayed the items that were to be its main elements—as well as some others that were eventually shifted into the higher education package or dropped altogether—at his session with Finch and Moynihan and again a week later when he heard them described to the Urban Affairs Council.

In January, he read a draft of the working group's proposed message, and in early February word came back that he approved it, save for a few changes and suggestions. He wanted a strong statement that diversity of schools and teaching methods make for better education. He wanted vigorous language, aimed at Catholic members of his "silent majority," that would highlight the importance of nonpublic schools. And, in a striking small paradigm of the sorts of things a president must consider, however little bearing they may seem to have on the subject at hand, he insisted that one statement critical of American education be toned down because it could possibly be used against the United States by unfriendly foreign governments. (The offending passage read: "We must stop congratulating ourselves for spending nearly as much money on education as does the entire rest of the world—$65 billion a year on all levels—when millions of our school children are denied an adequate opportunity to learn." The final version altered the subordinate clause to "when we are not getting as much as we should out of the dollars we spend.")

The president also received communications, by memorandum and in person, from senior aides such as Ehrlichman and Moynihan who dealt directly with him. Moynihan struck a responsive chord in Nixon with his account of the tone and rhetorical import of the message. As in welfare, both men felt that a conservative president was singularly well suited to proposing radical reform. Unlike welfare, the radicalism of the education message did not inhere in any ambitious new programs, but in the new analytical framework the president urged upon the nation. The notion that schools should produce learning, rather than simply absorb resources, is at one level so obvious that it is embarrassing to suggest that putting the idea into the president's mouth was even interesting, let alone novel. Yet if it had been implicit in the pronouncements of previous administrations—there must, after all, be some reason why another federal education program is worth having and that reason must have something to do with what children learn—it was Moynihan's view that three years after the Coleman Report the time had come for the president to be explicit: the nation should regard its schools, with or without federal dollars in them, in terms of their productivity. Granted the need to pay teachers a living wage, granted the Constitutional and moral uncertainty of spending more on some schools than on others, granted also the inadequacy of existing measures of pupil achievement, it was still important for the chief executive to rise in his bully pulpit and assert that "There is only one important question to be asked about education: What do the children learn?"

Nixon evidently found this stance congenial. He could announce himself in favor of education, but not necessarily of schools and educators, and therein lay the course of political expediency if not ultimate wisdom. James Allen periodically recalled for his staff the president's private comments during a rare audience with the new commissioner in mid-1969. When he and Earl Warren first ran for Congress from California, Nixon reminisced, "You ran on a platform of good roads and good schools." Now, said the chief executive two decades later, "You run on a platform in favor of education but against what is going on in the schools." When he told this story, Allen would always shake his head.

Omissions and Contradictions

The principal logical flaw and programmatic gap in the education message was clear to Moynihan and others on the working group who were acquainted with the full policy implications of the Coleman Report.

Of all the in-school variables that had some positive correlation with student achievement, the most significant was peer group—that is, the composition of the student body itself. The best thing a disadvantaged youngster could do—other than to acquire new parents at an early age—was to enroll in a school filled largely with middle- and upper-class youngsters.

This, in a word, was integration, an idea that appeared only once, toward the end of the education message, albeit in words both succinct and direct: "I am well aware," said the president, "that 'quality education' is already being interpreted as 'code words' for a delay of desegregation. We must never let that meaning take hold. Quality is what education is all about; desegregation is vital to that quality. . . ."

The educational value of integration revealed by the Coleman data was not necessarily a consequence of mixing black with white. Its essence lay in the combining of youngsters from different socioeconomic strata in the same schools and classrooms. Its benefit seemed to accrue to low-income students attending predominantly middle-class schools. That the nation's black population had a disproportionate share of youngsters from disadvantaged backgrounds and a distressingly small share of middle-class students implied that any meaningful integration by social class would necessarily cut across racial lines as well. But the effects of race *per se* were virtually impossible to disentangle statistically from other factors and, besides, did not make for a politically rewarding line of inquiry.

The effect of integration on pupil achievement was not great, particularly when compared with the powerful impact of family environment, but it appeared palpable enough that an output-driven conception of education that was mindful of the plight of the disadvantaged, while making short shrift of compensatory programs, could logically have led to a resounding endorsement of integration as a tool of national policy.

It did not. Others in the White House were simultaneously engaged, under the auspices of a Cabinet Committee on School Desegregation chaired by Vice President Spiro Agnew, in a complex attempt to blend the dictates of the federal courts with the perceived political realities of the Nixon administration in pursuit of a workable policy on school desegregation. (It was never thought of as "integration.") The first substantial result of that endeavor would be the president's lengthy statement of March 24, 1970, in which he reached for several objectives: to indicate that the administration, having decisively lost its courtroom attempts to slow the pace of desegregation, would henceforth obey the judges; simultaneously to transfer the political onus of desegregation from the executive branch, which had somehow to enforce these rulings, to the courts that handed them down; and to take some of the sting out of compliance by proposing new federal funds for school districts undergoing desegregation.[7]

This financial commitment—which would be enacted in altered form as the Emergency School Aid Act of 1972—addressed two presidential purposes: "programs for improving education in racially-impacted areas" and "assisting school districts in meeting special problems incident to court-ordered desegregation."[8] Although each objective may be thought laudable in its own right, taken together they smacked of trying to have it both ways and in view of the analysis of the education reform message, it was especially ironic that the first of these proposals in the desegregation statement came out sounding very much like more money for compensatory education. In Nixon's words, one of the four criteria by which the proposed funds—which he described as totaling $500 million in fiscal 1971 and a full billion the following year—would be allocated was to meet "the special needs of racially-impacted schools where *de facto* segregation persists—and where immediate injections of money can make a real difference in terms of educational effectiveness."[9]

If one were simply evaluating the nearly concurrent presidential statements on desegregation and "lower education" from the perspective of their appeal to an audience of liberal educators—which of course was not Nixon's main consideration—the juxtaposition could not have been worse. The education reform message decried the spending of additional money on popular existing programs that Congress was keen to expand, challenged the philosophic and scientific base on which compensatory education rested, insisted that research was needed before any infusion of money could be justified, and held the schools to a rigorous standard of productivity as the measure of their worth. The desegregation statement, on the other hand, talked of vast sums channelled through a new sort of compensatory program that could be viewed as a reward for keeping schools segregated. Not only were the two thrusts incompatible, neither was strictly true to the social science findings.

But analytic consistency is a lofty and seldom-achieved standard by which to gauge the actions and proposals of an entire administration, and it is significant that the membership of the groups that generated the two statements overlapped only a little. Each had been established for a different reason; the one to say something about education, the other to deal with the desegregation conundrum. Each wrote for the same president, but their purposes and outside audiences diverged.[b]

It would later be argued, by Moynihan among others, that the administration's use of the honey of presidential sympathy and federal funds, alongside the familiar vinegar of court orders and aid cutoffs, did make school desegregation more palatable in the south and contributed to the progress those states made in eliminating *de jure* segregation during the Nixon years. Certainly the president's

---

[b]It may be noted that Nixon personally drafted much of the desegregation statement.

show of understanding, including his conciliatory visit to New Orleans in August 1970, helped ease tensions that might otherwise have built in southern cities as the courts disallowed open enrollment and moved toward less voluntary means of desegregation. The administration's insistence on treating the heavily—if mostly *de facto*—segregated north the same as the much-abused south also fed the appearance of fairness. The results, in any case, were encouraging: "Unitary" school systems in the south, which were rare in 1968 had become, at least on paper, commonplace by 1970. This historic accomplishment is not erased by pointing out that trying to soften the blow, to put the onus on the courts, and to chide the north as well, all fit nicely into the administration's so-called "southern strategy."

In this context, it is not surprising that the education reform message stopped short of urging the integration of schools by social class, even if doing so would have been consistent with the Coleman-based analysis that the president otherwise espoused. But to accede, within a few short weeks, to a desegregation strategy that incorporated the logic of compensatory spending, while understandable in its own terms, nevertheless detracted from the integrity of the first message and showed that this administration, like others, could devise somewhat inconsistent solutions for overlapping problems, depending in part on the political stakes and on who in the White House was working on what.

Higher Education

Until November 1969, those working on the Nixon administration's education policies expected the president's eventual Message to Congress to span the subject from kindergarten to graduate school. Three of the six points in the seminal Moynihan-Finch memorandum that the president had read with approbation on October tenth pertained to higher education, and the message's early versions were drafted accordingly.

By late October, however, some participants had begun to worry that the message was coming to resemble a Christmas tree. Budget Bureau Director Robert Mayo, at Nathan's urging, recommended that no education message be sent at all, but that if one were it should be trimmed down to include only the administration's strongest and best-developed proposals.

At a meeting in John Ehrlichman's office on November fifth, this viewpoint prevailed, and it was decided to confine the message then under preparation to the two central recommendations for elementary and secondary education, set in the ringing rhetorical context of "reform." Higher education was shelved until such time as the administration's plans for it could be shaped more carefully.

Within days, however, it became clear that events would not afford much leisure for that process. The White House was reminded of a provision in the 1968 Education Amendments in which Congress had mandated the president to report by December 1969 on the feasibility of providing "universal higher education." In fact, an interdepartmental group had been quietly at work on this study since spring, but by November it appeared to Commissioner Allen, Secretary Finch, and the Budget Bureau staff that the emerging report was not very good. Moreover, Representative Edith Green, chairman of the House Special Subcommittee on Education, was reportedly ready to introduce her own omnibus higher education bill. In addition, HEW's fiscal 1971 budget submission and its proposed legislative package for the 1970 congressional session included several new higher education provisions that were hard for the Executive Office even to weigh in the absence of an overall administration policy.

Clearly the time had come to assemble a group to review the existing higher education programs and to consider the president's options for the future.

It was natural that Edward L. Morgan would take on the task of organizing a new working group for higher education, since most of its members would be persons already active in the elementary and secondary task force, and since most of the current program ideas were legacies of October's effort to deal with both levels together.

At an initial session in Allen's office on November twenty-sixth, everyone agreed that the commissioner would speedily write the first draft of a statement on higher education policy, chiefly as a way of getting a viewpoint and program framework down on paper so that others would have a common starting point.

Bernard Martin of the Budget Bureau and I started writing staff memoranda summarizing key higher education policy issues for the nascent working group. Martin Kramer, the higher education specialist on Butler's staff, set out to pen language for Allen. A policy brushfire flared up in early December when, for the third time in recent years, the Senate passed a tax credit for college tuition payments, and Arthur Burns urged the president to endorse the idea in his forthcoming State of the Union Message. In campaign speeches, Nixon had favored such tax credits, but now, with the rest of his advisers united in opposition to the idea, with the annual message devoted mainly to environmental matters and with no chance that Wilbur Mills would let such a plan through the Ways and Means Committee anyway, the notion made little headway in the White House.

In mid-December, with Commissioner Allen's draft statement in hand, Morgan reconvened the new higher education working group, and by Christmas it was meeting regularly.[a] The decision to commence by framing a presidential Message to Congress, rather than by taking up the policy issues the group was beginning to lay out, was a questionable procedure, for it saddled the participants with rhetoric before the content of the message took shape. And the substantive issues were both fundamental and intricate. Unlike elementary and secondary education, there was no presumption here that most existing programs would endure unchanged. To the contrary, the working group sensed that this was a rare opportunity to review and possibly recast the basic legislation that fixed the relationship between Washington and the nation's colleges and universities, at least insofar as the USOE programs determined that relationship. Also in contrast to elementary and secondary education, no one saw federal policy as peripheral to decisions made at the state and local level. Washington had a much larger stake in the nation's postsecondary enterprise and its actions could powerfully affect the basic shape and direction of that enterprise. Moreover, whereas the "lower education" working group began with most of its basic policy directions already ratified by the Urban Affairs Council and the president, the higher education panel realized that it had the opportunity to go back to fundamentals and the responsibility to present Nixon with a fully considered package of alternatives.

---

[a]As Morgan had asked Allen to have his draft ready by December fifteenth, I was startled to receive an urgent summons that morning to meet with the commissioner after lunch. My wonder grew when it developed that he wanted me to ghost a draft for him. Flattering though it was to be asked, it was also a poignant and discouraging sign of the poverty of USOE's staff resources that the commissioner of education had to request a junior White House aide to lend a hand. Nevertheless, I gave it a try and was naturally pleased, if again bemused to discover, when Allen circulated "his" version a few days later, that nearly all of it consisted of my words.

The Policy Context

The expiring higher education programs administered by the Office of Education were a grab bag of student aid and categorical support schemes. Much of the money that they dispensed went to help individuals meet the costs of attending college, but in spite of a general tendency to channel these funds to low-income students, there had never been a clear decision as to which parts of the population should be eligible for federal assistance. Programs had arisen at different times and were addressed to diverse purposes, resulting in a bewildering array of grant, loan, and job schemes, varied subsidy rates, erratic criteria for participation, and inconsistent formulae for distributing the funds. Nor had the emphasis on student aid done away with another set of programs—construction grants and loans, library aid, teacher training provisions, and the like—that made federal funds available to colleges and universities for institutional purposes.

Although no one in the Nixon White House was more than barely aware of it, one of the last acts of the Johnson administration had been the preparation of a comprehensive study of higher education policy. Just two weeks before inauguration day, HEW Secretary Wilbur J. Cohen signed off on the report that had been prepared in his department by a team headed by Alice M. Rivlin, assistant secretary for planning and evaluation. The Rivlin Report, as it was known, clearly posed the choice between student assistance and institutional aid and judged the former to be "a more effective mechanism for promoting equality of educational opportunity," while money given directly to the colleges would be preferable if the goal were to increase "resources per student."[1]

Acknowledging the links between the two types of aid, Rivlin and her associates nevertheless chose to stress equal opportunity, and therefore proposed a package of grants and subsidized loans for needy students. The goal they adduced, "ensuring that all able students can afford to go on to higher education" was not new. The National Defense Education Act of 1958 had stated its objective in almost identical language—"programs that will give assurance that no student of ability will be denied an opportunity for higher education because of financial need"—and John Kennedy had echoed the same principle in a Message to Congress in 1963.

Yet the goal had not been attained. The Rivlin panel enumerated the problems: because the principal programs were "campus-based," a low-income student's access to federal assistance hinged on his admission to particular colleges; the maximum scholarship amounts were small and the availability of loans to augment them was discouragingly uneven; the several programs were ill synchronized; subsidies were not well-"targetted" on the neediest students; and overall appropriations were too small to fulfill the programs' promise.

The recently-formed Carnegie Commission on Higher Education issued its first policy statement in December 1968, foreshadowing by a few weeks many of the proposals of the Rivlin Report.[2] Nixon's own "transition task force" on education, headed by the Carnegie Corporation's Alan Pifer, while divided in its recommendations was unanimous in its finding that existing student aid programs failed to provide equal opportunity. In that cloudy way by which a working consensus emerges on issues of public policy, one could detect agreement that the federal government had a proper role in ensuring that access to a college education was not denied people on account of poverty, that the existing *pot pourri* of programs did not adequately discharge that responsibility, and that the time had come to consider necessary changes. It is one of the small ironies of recent history that it fell to a conservative Republican president to grapple with this progressive set of propositions.

Aid to Institutions

Helping poverty-stricken students to pay for college is not the same as helping colleges to meet their payrolls, and in the troubled years of the late sixties, the latter notion weighed on the minds of those charged with maintenance of the nation's postsecondary institutions. The condition that Earl Cheit was to dub the "New Depression" in higher education had arrived, as one campus after another experienced deficit budgets and saw worse trouble ahead.[3]

Colleges wanting help turned to Washington as the only source with the means to deal with financial problems of this magnitude. The American Council on Education, the umbrella organization of colleges and universities, announced in 1969 that "the principal unfinished business of the Federal Government in the field of higher education is the necessity to provide support for general institutional purposes."[4] Additional funds for categorical programs already on the books were also needed, but these alone would not suffice, for "the financial situation of our colleges and universities had steadily deteriorated." The time had come, the institutional spokesmen were convinced, for a quantum jump in the terms of federal support for higher education, for a broadening of the definition of Washington's role to include a commitment to the well-being of the colleges themselves.

Excellence and Reform

Whatever it is that constitutes "quality" in American higher education had, in ways nearly as impalpable as the criteria themselves, also begun to worry some academic leaders.

In part this was simply a consequence of fiscal belt tightening. The Association of American Universities, the spokesman for the nation's leading research institutions, warned that the kinds of retrenchment underway on the campus threatened "the slow stifling of higher education as a vital, creative, productive force in American life."[5] The National Science Board detected a "rapidly increasing disparity between the financial resources of most institutions of higher learning and the expectations of American society."[6] The growth of the higher education system had been so rapid, the Carnegie Commission cautioned, that any shrinkage of resources in the face of continuing urgent need to make room for students seeking admission would force a brutal choice between "quality" and "equality."

A more subtle question was whether the economic woes of particular universities foreshadowed a decline in the caliber of scholarship that, in the postwar decades, had pushed the United States to the forefront of world research, technological prowess, and intellectual attainment. This was not a subject easily assayed, both because measures were elusive and because no one in the academy much wanted to concede that his own institution was flagging. But the well-publicized deficits of a few major research universities, the consequences of the levelling off in government research support, the absolute decline in federal graduate fellowships and traineeships after their 1968 peak, the susceptibility of elite universities to student disturbance, the punitive mood in the legislatures as students rioted, and a new onslaught of anti-intellectualism on the campus itself all contributed to a sense that academic quality hung in the balance.

Traditional notions of educational excellence were also under assault from another direction. Reform was in the air. Its broad banner waved over causes as diverse as student participation in faculty selection, improved undergraduate instruction, the granting of academic credit for "real life experience," and the creation of new and "relevant" fields of study. Its proponents ranged from angry students to solemn commissions. What united them was a vague sense that American higher education was somehow getting out of date. Innovation, many thought, was urgently needed.

The Campus Condition

In a May 1970 Gallup poll, more Americans deemed campus unrest the gravest problem facing the nation than cited racial strife, the Vietnam War, or the high cost of living. Gardner Ackley termed the last twelve months of the nineteen-sixties "a tragic year in the life of the University of Michigan—a year that has begun the destruction of this university as a great center of learning."[7] The Carnegie Commission intoned that "The campuses have, in recent years, been in the greatest turmoil in all their history of over three centuries." One fifth of the nation's colleges and universities were shut down for a day or longer in the spring of 1970. Twenty-eight percent of public universities experienced violent or destructive demonstrations. In two years, twenty state legislatures passed laws making various forms of campus misbehavior into criminal offenses.[9]

The Vietnam War was probably the most important factor, particularly as felt by students subject to the draft or angered by the presence of ROTC on campus. The urban riots of the several previous summers, the spate of political assassinations, and the politicization of university communities all fanned the flames. Whatever the causes, dissent and disruption on the campus had become a major national issue that would inevitably color any review of federal post-secondary policy.

In a sense, it already had. Protest had not stayed behind the ivied walls. It had come to Washington in the form of giant antiwar marches and demonstrations that plagued the final years of the Johnson administration and, by the autumn of 1969, beset the Nixon White House as well. On November 15, the White House complex was surrounded by D.C. Transit buses, parked nose to tail. Armed troops were concealed in the Treasury Department and the Executive Office Building. To be sure, education policy had little to do with the angry speeches and obscene chants heard on the Ellipse. Nor were all of the protestors college students. Yet in the crowd and among those within the barricades, there was a sense of rising hostility between the federal government and the higher education community.

The Interests of the Working Group

The task force that Edward L. Morgan convened in his cavernous office in the old Executive Office Building contained a fair cross-section of the higher education policy issues and concerns then abroad in the nation. He was perhaps the only one in the room without an agenda or preconception of his own but speedily familiarized himself with the principal issues and with the predilections of those he would be working with so closely in the coming weeks. To the end, he remained steadfast in his neutrality, however, and proved to be an excellent chairman.

Daniel P. Moynihan, by late 1969 a "Counselor to the President" and member of the cabinet, was the ranking person present, even if he no longer had operational responsibility for White House policy development. He was also by some margin the most eloquent and persuasive member of the working group.

Having skillfully led the president in the early weeks of the administration to a noninterventionist stance on campus unrest and having kept the presidency opposed to congressional attempts to punish disruptive students, he fervently wanted to have this position codified in a Message to Congress that would define and defend academic freedom, pledge the executive branch—and in time, perhaps the entire government—to maintain its hands-off policy, and propose steps to strengthen the ability of universities to manage their own affairs.

Moynihan's other consuming interest was the threat to scholarly excellence in the prestigious research universities that were running out of money, beseiged by their own students, and seemingly less esteemed by the society.

These ideas converged in his mind, blending liberalism with elitism and federal restraint with governmental activism. Part of the presidential advisor's motivation stemmed from his general dismay at the substitution of formal constraints for the ancient self-regulating norms that he deemed essential to the survival of democratic society. He had as little patience with college administrators fingering Washington for their inability to maintain open discourse on the campuses as he had with politicians seeking to impose controls on the academy. How, he wondered, could the high-quality, dispassionate scholarship that nourished the nation prosper in a politicized atmosphere of abuse, regulation, and suspicion?

Science Advisor Lee A. DuBridge shared many of these concerns. The former president of the California Institute of Technology, he held much the same conception of academic freedom and excellence as the Harvard professor, possibly strengthened by his long immersion in the "hard" sciences that figured so prominently in Washington's relations with the academy. Advanced research in fields such as particle physics demanded outstanding scholars, ample funds, and an atmosphere free from distraction.

With research went graduate training. With both, in DuBridge's mind, went the need to support the colleges and universities themselves, for they were the source of scholarship and instruction and had fallen on hard times. Yet his conception of the proper federal role in higher education was even broader than that. Curriculum reform also interested him, as did the need to build community colleges and strengthen the society's capacity to provide technical and vocational training to those for whom a classical liberal arts education was unsuited. Ample financial aid was also needed if low-income persons were not to be barred from postsecondary schooling. The only member of the working group who had actually run a university, DuBridge's own agenda for federal higher education policy perhaps came closest to spanning all the yearnings of the academy.

Herbert Stein represented the Council of Economic Advisors. Since all three of the council's members at the time were former university professors, their perspective on higher education policy was broader than the institutional role of the CEA might suggest. But Stein's particular interest, and the special strength he brought to the discussions, was in meshing program options with sound economic doctrine. Not surprisingly, he espoused the view that postsecondary schooling is an investment, that those who receive it will become less disadvantaged, that it is therefore reasonable to rely heavily on loans in financing higher education, that the government should limit its outright student subsidies, and that the colleges themselves should not receive direct federal payments for educational purposes (though they could be paid for other services rendered) but should instead be obliged to operate in the student marketplace.

The Department of Health, Education and Welfare spoke with two voices in the higher education working group, as on elementary and secondary education. The main spokesmen were the same; Assistant Secretary Lewis Butler representing the departmental perspective, and Commissioner James E. Allen, Jr., that of the Office of Education.

Butler had inherited the Rivlin Report and much of the staff that produced it. He also absorbed many of the assumptions of veteran HEW higher education policy analysts such as Martin Kramer. Four ideas were central: the time had come to build coherence into federal higher education policy, with the emphasis on programs already lodged by statute in HEW; aid should go to students rather than institutions; it should be parcelled out so as to help primarily those low-income persons whose poverty might otherwise bar them from college; and Washington should use its leverage to open up higher education to a less-cramped definition of its mission and to a broader assortment of institutions, curricula, and pedagogies. The emphasis on reform would grow stronger, as the Newman Task Force—which Butler had much to do with initiating and which included two of his key aides—worked toward its conclusions, but the idea was already there. Hardly a radical, Butler was a reformer at heart who found few federal activities that were operating in an optimal manner and few institutions in society that would not benefit from a nudge. As a lawyer, he was free from professional entanglements with the higher education establishment, and he had little patience with academic cant, scant sympathy for unexamined traditionalism, and a splendid sense of humor.

Allen, by contrast, led the agency that ran many of the existing programs, and was unavoidably regarded by most educators as their representative in the executive branch. Like it or not, his office therefore focused both the interests of the bureaucracy and the demands and concerns of the outside constituency.

In his quiet, gentlemanly way, the commissioner was also a reformer who saw in the nation's higher education enterprise much that he hoped to improve. But his brand of reform would have been more welcome in the White House of the New Frontier or the Great Society, for it started with the assumption that the resources being devoted to higher education were inadequate, that augmenting them was a precondition of changing the system, and that much of the responsibility for providing the additional funds should be assumed by Washington. He was visibly uneasy with the notion that monies expended in the name of education might be thought wasted or that Washington's interest in higher education might be something other than the health and happiness of the system as defined by its more thoughtful professional practitioners.

A passionate believer in equal opportunity, Allen championed the idea that the first responsibility of the federal government was to break down the legal, financial, and conceptual barriers that kept the poor and the black from obtaining as much education as the prosperous and white. But he favored outright subsidies rather than loans, for his version of the investment theory of higher education had the returns accruing to the society as well as to the individual. He also felt that colleges and universities deserved operating subsidies so that they could afford to grow, to change, and to provide the quality instruction all their students sought.

The Bureau of the Budget characteristically saw matters through different lenses. Assistant Director Richard Nathan and his education staff had views on higher education policy that reflected both their own ideas and their institutional obligation. Although the Budget Bureau frequently gets cast as the heavy in any White House policy drama—and its representatives dare not forget their responsibility for guarding the "bottom line" of the president's budget—it oversimplifies its role to construe the Bureau as simply opposed to ideas that cost money. Budget examiners pride themselves on their nonideological adaptability and professionalism. Insofar as they can make out what the president wants, they will conduct themselves accordingly. But the Bureau nurtures some distinctive attitudes toward government, too, and if there is no clear guidance from the White House to the contrary, these will influence the positions of Budget representatives in policy deliberations.

Perhaps the strongest god in its pantheon is effectiveness, the proposition that government should undertake only those tasks it is competent to handle and should spend whatever resources it can muster in ways that have the greatest assurance of success. Although Budget Bureau staff members had taken part in the development of the social programs of the 1960s, by decade's end their skepticism was mounting. Responding also to the Nixon administration's evident contempt for "narrow categorical programs," the political appointees and senior career employees of BOB came to suspect that the proliferation of such programs fomented waste while committing Washington to inflexible funding arrangements that could seldom be altered or withdrawn regardless of changed conditions or priorities. They were growing wary of supporting institutions directly, sensing that the clients, once adopted, would never be dislodged and that such unquestioning assistance fostered heedless spending among the recipients. They were also dubious of programs that bestow complex decisions and wide discretion on federal officials, because of the bureaucracy's tendency to enlarge itself and to be captured by constituents and turned into advocates for their programs.

Richard Nathan was rapidly becoming the administration's most articulate spokesman for the philosophy known as the "New Federalism." As already manifest in the president's proposals for welfare reform, manpower training, and revenue sharing, this was a more complex idea than simply giving discretionary funds to states and localities to spend as they liked. Underlying it was the proposition that the nation's federal structure had been bent and that public functions needed to be reassigned to the levels of government best able to handle them. Many programs heretofore run directly out of Washington might better be managed by jurisdictions more sensitive to local conditions. The national government, on the other hand, was uniquely adept at collecting and distributing money. Hence welfare payments might properly be federalized, for here state discretion had produced clear inequities. But most direct services were better left to state and local governments to deliver, perhaps with a financial boost from Washington, which in turn could purge itself of undertakings doomed to ham-handedness if assayed from the banks of the Potomac.

Higher education made an interesting test of this philosophy, but one that Budget Bureau officials found ultimately consistent with the New Federalism and its twin, the "income strategy." Low-income students, like poverty-stricken families, needed money, and Washington was competent to distribute it to them. Colleges and universities, on the other hand, were creatures of the states and the private sector and should not be allowed to become direct federal clients. Yet the federal government retained an interest in the adequacy of the "delivery system" and should engineer its programs in ways likely to promote reform and renewal. But the Budget Bureau had even less confidence in the Office of Education than in most Washington agencies and therefore favored mechanisms for reform that left little discretion in the hands of OE bureaucrats.

The least expected push for higher education reform in the working group came from the Department of Labor. Its origins lay not so much in that agency's institutional predilections—although the widening gap between the nation's manpower needs and the interests of the traditional higher education community certainly played a part—as in the personal views of two key persons. Labor Secretary George Shultz was an educator, formerly dean of the University of Chicago Graduate School of Business. Although he did not personally sit in the working group, he was ably represented there by Assistant Secretary (for Policy, Evaluation and Research) Jerome M. Rosow, who turned out to be a staunch advocate of change and renewal in higher education. A graduate of the University of Chicago, Rosow's career had been spent primarily in the oil industry. Like Lew Butler, his perceptions may have been especially acute and uninhibited because he had no formal ties with the education profession. Beginning with a long paper he wrote for Shultz in September 1969 entitled "Restructuring Undergraduate Education as a Key Aspect of Coping with Student Unrest" and continuing well past the working group's deliberations, Rosow was, in his quiet, self-effacing way, perhaps the most ardent reformer of higher education in the Nixon cabinet and subcabinet. Characteristically, he began his commentary on Commissioner Allen's initial draft with the observation "that the message needs an additional dimension which conveys the President's awareness that a crisis has developed with regard to the future of higher education, involving financing, governance, teaching, curricula and students' career direction, and that reform is urgently needed."

Another sometime participant in the working group deserves mention, also, not because his views prevailed but because of their nature. Roger A. Freeman, formerly (and subsequently) a scholar at Stanford's Hoover Institution on War, Revolution and Peace, was a long-time critic of direct federal aid to education and one of the nation's foremost proponents of the income tax credit approach. As it happened, the Joint Economic Committee published a particularly cogent paper on this subject by Freeman in mid-autumn 1969, as the working group was getting underway and just a few weeks before the Senate approved a tax credit scheme.[10] It was Freeman who urged Arthur Burns to recommend presidential endorsement of the idea, and Freeman who penned lengthy critiques of working group drafts embodying other ideas. There is no way of knowing what influence he might have had if his mentor had remained at the White House, but with Burns' departure for the Federal Reserve Board at the end of 1969, Freeman no longer had much claim to be heeded. In time, Morgan tired of his single-minded devotion to a position that no one else on the working group shared and eventually simply stopped inviting him to meetings and circulating papers to him. A few months later, Freeman returned to Palo Alto, and tax credits did not appear in the president's higher education message.

The Policy Process

The comments that Allen's first draft elicited from working group members served to isolate the principal issues that would be taken up and also helped each participant to take the measure of his colleagues. On January 8, 1970, Morgan convened the group, listened to everyone's leading ideas, and assigned tasks.

A week later, the final report of the Hester Task Force arrived at the White House.[11] Chaired by the president of New York University, this blue-ribbon panel was another of Arthur Burns' legacies to his colleagues, one of the many such groups he had organized in late 1969 to obtain informed counsel on important domestic policy issues. This entire exercise can be seen on at least three levels: as a public relations ploy, designed to give dozens of prestigious outsiders a sense of participation in the work of the Nixon administration; as a replay of Johnson's strategy of appointing prominent experts to define for the White House a sort of working consensus on what should be done about particular areas of national concern; and as a tactical maneuver by Burns and his staff to retrieve some of the domestic policy initiative that had been lost to Moynihan's Urban Affairs Council. But Burns' absence when the task force reports came in, and Ehrlichman's ascendancy, doomed most of these documents to sit on the shelf, save perhaps where their recommendations chanced to mesh with what various working groups and other domestic advisors wanted to do anyway.

In the case of higher education, the Hester panel was all but ignored. The task force had worked with commendable speed, and its report was a model of clarity but, perhaps because most of its members were college presidents, it was couched in the rhetoric of ever larger federal outlays for higher education, with emphasis on the need to sustain colleges and universities *qua* institutions. Although several of its specific recommendations corresponded closely to ideas Moynihan and DuBridge were advancing and although it enthusiastically backed the expansion of aid to disadvantaged students as well, in the White House it was read as special pleading by a client group more concerned with its own welfare than with the public interest. If that characterization was unfair to its substantive proposals, no one on the Morgan group much cared, for the rousing cry for more money was bound to embarrass an administration that was seeking to hone the federal role to greater effectiveness without a precipitous increase in expenditures. Once released, the Hester Report would strengthen the hand of those whose main goal was bigger appropriations and who faulted the administration for spending too little on education. Hence not only was the report ignored—although Hester and Morgan had an amiable conversation about it—it was actually suppressed for a time, not being published by the Government Printing Office until August, long after the administration's proposals were public.

The working group members went about their tasks in January and eyed a tentative March deadline for the Message to Congress. Then pressure to expedite the message began to build. The condition on many campuses was deteriorating. Higher education hearings had started in the House in December and were to commence in the Senate in early February. The minority staff director of the Senate Labor and Public Welfare Committee wrote to White House legislative liaison man Bryce Harlow urging speed, and HEW's Charles B. Saunders voiced similar concerns. Morgan responded by rescheduling some working group meetings to try to get an earlier consensus on policy contents, but the issues proved knottier than he and his associates anticipated, and it was to be March nineteenth before the message finally went to Congress.

The weeks in between were hectic, with so many simultaneous developments, that the key options and decisions can be grasped more easily if the major topics are considered separately as in the following sections.

Student Financial Aid

The administration's policy review of student aid actually commenced well before January. The statutory requirement of an executive branch report on access to higher education had pushed the subject to the fore, at least within HEW, for most of 1969. During the summer, the legal ceiling on interest rates for federally guaranteed student loans had also become an issue, as other interest rates soared so high that bankers no longer found it attractive to lend to students. At that point, adopting a position favored by the Treasury Department and its banking constituency, the president urged and Congress enacted a "special allowance" whereby the government would pay an extra premium allowing lenders to get their customary interest without students having to bear a usurious burden.

That sequence had highlighted a central problem in federal student loan programs, which was the reluctance of private lenders to put much capital into them. Student loans were individually small, involved much paperwork, had no collateral, were uncommonly prone to default, and had that interest rate limit, which, in combination with the long repayment period, posed risks that prudent bankers would just as soon avoid. Hence Washington was bombarded with reports that banks were denying student loan applications, save for their regular customers, and that low- and middle-income persons were finding it especially hard to borrow, notwithstanding the federal guarantee.

One way to address this problem was by establishing a "secondary market" for student loans, wherein private lenders—colleges and banks alike—might sell their commitments to a quasi-governmental corporation, much as home mortgages are sold to "Fannie Mae," and thereby replenish their liquid reserves. Advocates of this scheme assumed not only that bankers would be more willing to engage in student loans in the knowledge that they need not keep their capital tied up for decades, but also that the volume of student loans would increase when lenders were helped to "recycle" their money.

It was an appealing idea, particularly for an administration that sought to make the fullest use of loans as an instrument of student aid policy, for—aside from any interest subsidies and default payments—such an arrangement could be kept "off the budget" yet serve as a valuable boost to students' ability to pay for college. But before it could emerge in March as a bill to create a "National Student Loan Association" this idea underwent protracted debate within the working group, not only because a credit market device of this sort is inherently complex, but also because the deliberations touched on weighty philosophical questions about Washington's role in student assistance.

For several years, a proposal had kicked around for the federal government to create an "Educational Opportunity Bank" to make student loans that would be repaid on an income-contingent basis—that is, repayment levels would vary with income, which meant that the actual burden of replenishing the loan fund would be borne in a progressive manner.[12] The Carnegie Commission had endorsed this idea.[13] The Rivlin task force had advocated a National Student Loan Bank, but without the income-contingent feature.[14] These various proposals had in common the notion that the government would loan money directly to students—which would mean that banks and other private lenders need not even be involved—but that actual federal subsidies would be confined to administrative costs, default guarantees and, perhaps, payment of interest while the student was in school. Such loans would be available to all students, regardless of income level, while special subsidies for impoverished students would be handled through separate need-based grant programs.

The working group initially found the loan bank idea attractive, but further exploration revealed three pitfalls. Those who believe that higher education benefits the society, and that society should therefore pay for it, naturally dislike heavy reliance on student loans, and the smaller the overt subsidy programs and larger the emphasis on loans the less they like it. Most "liberal" versions of the loan bank idea, therefore, including the Carnegie Commission and Rivlin approaches, construed the bank as a supplement to substantial federal outlays for need-based scholarships. Even in that form, it had few admirers in public higher education, whose leaders saw in it an invitation for colleges to hike their tuition charges and for states to shrink their institutional subsidies.

Second, because the loan bank would be a new public agency in the direct lending field and because its access to government security markets and federal guarantees enabled it to raise capital and make loans at "bargain" rates, private lenders did not like it. They feared it would take over a goodly portion of their business, which they claimed could easily handle the demand for student loans if only the government would create a secondary market for the loan paper—quite a different idea than Washington serving as a direct lender.

Third, the new bank might get a great deal of business—no one could say exactly how much, but estimates ranged well into the billions—which would force it to sop up vast sums from the capital market. This meant less resources available for other public and private purposes, added pressure on the money supply and on interest rates, and a distortion of accustomed flows of capital and credit. As Herbert Stein posed the issue to the working group, "The fact that we may think that loans are a good way to put resources *into* education does not imply that borrowing is a good way to take resources *out of* the rest of the economy." Such considerations transcended questions of federal subsidies and on- versus off-the-budget financing—matters that other working group members were more at home with—and invaded the higher reaches of national economic policy.

These issues generated much debate within the working group and elsewhere in the executive branch. Although the income contingent feature was never taken seriously, a form of "low-income insurance" stayed under active consideration well into February. It was featured in the HEW loan plan as presented by Butler, who envisioned phasing out the program of National Defense Student Loans, merging it with the Guaranteed Loan Program, and putting both in the hands of a new federal agency that would combine the functions of a "secondary market" with the ability to function simultaneously as a direct lender. Washington would subsidize the interest on loans to students from low-income families, but all other borrowing would be at "market rates" and the entire enterprise would be "off the budget" save for the subsidies, with even the low-income insurance being financed through borrower premiums rather than general revenues.

This scheme came under fire from HEW's own Office of Legislation. Deputy Assistant Secretary Charles B. Saunders, Jr. warned Morgan that "The proposal to shift the major cost burden for higher education to the individual student is a formula for political disaster." He predicted bitter opposition from the higher education lobby, especially the spokesmen for public colleges, and even from Republicans in Congress.

Nor did the Office of Education favor the bank idea. Commissioner Allen wanted the NDSL program retained, complete with interest subsidies (although he advanced an intricate scheme for raising some of its capital from private rather than federal sources) and a secondary market created to service lenders under the Guaranteed Loan Program. His principal concern, however, was with expanding scholarships and other forms of direct student subsidies.

The Treasury Department weighed in with a scathing critique of the loan bank idea and urged instead nothing more than a secondary market for loans that would, presumably, continue to be made largely by private lenders. Some members of the working group suspected Treasury of greater concern for the interests of bankers than those of college students—a suspicion heightened by the fact that Undersecretary Charls E. Walker, from whose office the memoranda came, though a distinguished public official, had been a top executive of the American Bankers Association before joining the administration. Nevertheless, the risk of dislocations in the capital markets was not one that many in the Morgan group felt qualified to deny.

Thus discussions proceeded at several levels and on overlapping issues. To what extent could students be helped to attend college without a heavy added burden on the federal budget? Budget Bureau representatives favored any scheme that reduced subsidies and kept outlays "off the budget," but the Bureau was not of one mind, since considerations of economic policy were also a responsibility it shared with Treasury and the CEA.

To whom should federal interest subsidies go? Most working group members preferred to focus them on students from the poorest families, but Commissioner Allen wanted to extend them more broadly, and the signals from Capitol Hill indicated that any proposal to scrap the popular Defense Loan program would not find favor with Congress.

Should Washington lend directly to students, or should that function be left to the banks and colleges that had traditionally discharged it? A full-blown federal commitment to an Educational Opportunity Bank would be a revolutionary initiative with profound consequences for society's assumptions about who should go to college and how it should be financed. As Lee DuBridge cautioned his colleagues, "The establishment of such a bank is a policy decision of the first magnitude, involving ultimately tens of billions of dollars and fundamental changes in higher education."

Slowly the working group moved toward agreement on student aid. The government would not become a direct lender but would establish a secondary market to make loans more readily available to students seeking them. The new outlet for loan paper would encourage the colleges and universities themselves to serve as lenders, thereby enhancing their ability to "package" student aid of all kinds. They would likely take a more generous view of student eligibility than did the banks, though these would also remain in the program and be able to patronize the secondary market. Instead of "low-income insurance" to make borrowing less fearsome to impoverished students, there would be separate subsidies for the needy, but these would not be built into the guaranteed loan program, which instead would be open to all students willing to pay full market interest rates.

The next questions, logically, were who should get those other subsidies and in what amounts? Most federal programs with "means tests" provide their largest benefits to the poorest recipients and reduce the sums as eligible participants move up the income scale. In such calculations there is a phase-out point—that is, an income level at which the federal benefit falls to zero and to which everyone below it is presumably being raised.

In student aid calculations, however, a second independent variable enters: the uneven costs of various kinds of postsecondary education. Two similarly situated families find themselves with quite different financing burdens if one is sending a child to a low-tuition community college while the other has elected a high-priced private university.

One way to accommodate this problem was for Washington to parcel its student aid monies among the colleges and universities themselves, allowing them to tailor assistance packages for individual students. That was the approach favored in the mid-sixties when the major Office of Education programs were established, and it continued to be popular among campus administrators, for it gave them custody of the government's funds and afforded considerable leeway in helping their students.

But "campus-based" aid had drawbacks, too. It insulated the colleges from market pressures they would feel if Washington's money went directly to the students, and in a time when responsiveness to student desires was increasingly deemed desirable for universities and government programs alike, it sustained an older and more paternalistic approach. It meant that a prospective student had no way of knowing how much federal assistance he might receive until some college had accepted him and reviewed his aid application. Worse, from the federal standpoint, it fostered inequities in the distribution of public funds. Impoverished students at one campus could be denied federal aid while their less needy brethren at another institution received it. The same person might get a larger stipend at one school than he would obtain at another. Two students from identical economic circumstances attending equally priced colleges could receive different amounts of federal assistance.

Hence the White House working group had also to consider the possibility of a "direct" federal program that would vouchsafe the same resource level to similarly situated students no matter where they enrolled. This was the preferred approach of the Rivlin Report, which had urged a nationwide scholarship program with a maximum grant of $1,500.[15] It was also embodied in the Carnegie Commission's proposal for a national "educational opportunity grant" program based strictly on student need as determined by family income levels.[16]

Most of the serious analysis of student aid options for the working group was done in Assistant Secretary Butler's office in HEW. His staff's goal was to mold four different forms of assistance—grants, work-study benefits, subsidized loans, and market-rate loans—into a single rational package that would get the most mileage out of the available "subsidy budget" without denying less-needy students access to resources, if only through borrowing. Although the idea of a direct relationship between Washington and the individual student had some appeal, Butler's analysts were reluctant to dispense with the proven ability of campus aid administrators to weave several strands of assistance into patterns suited to each student's circumstances. Instead, they reasoned, Washington would fix ceilings on eligible income levels and would further specify points within the eligibility range where one kind of subsidy would phase out and another come into play. Thus the government would in fact guarantee a certain resource level to every needy student, but the "delivery system," at least for the subsidized programs, would continue to be the colleges and universities.

Probably no one in the working group save Butler fully apprehended the details of this intricate scheme. Nor did anyone try to second guess him, for it required sophisticated staff work, computer analysis, and detailed understanding of student income levels, the workings of existing programs, and the costs of various postsecondary institutions. For others in the room, three bits of information sufficed: the family income level at which the final dollar of federal subsidy would vanish; the maximum assistance available to the lowest-income student; and the budgetary consequences of various combinations of the first two figures.

A key factor in these deliberations was that in some unstated but important way, Butler and his staff were trusted. Others in the working group had relied heavily on him during the even more complicated formulation of the welfare reform program the previous summer. He had a gift for translating arcane analysis into policy options that politically astute laymen could grasp, and he did his homework with care.

The only other approach to student aid that the working group entertained was one Allen brought from the Office of Education, and the skepticism which greeted that scheme further assured Butler's domination of the final package. The Allen plan was eloquent in its assertion of goals, socially progressive in its underlying philosophy, and presented in terms that educators would find congenial, but somehow its analytical level was missing. Participation rates and costs appeared to be based more on hunches and assumptions than on computer runs. Funding mechanisms for the several parts of the plan, while individually imaginative, were not integrated. And the policy choices were unclear. Allen and his aides were not able to say with any precision what would happen at different appropriations levels, how much would have to be budgeted to ensure that persons of a given income level received stated amounts of aid, and so forth.

In trying to win support for his version, Allen faced two basic problems. No one on the working group was prepared to accept his assertions without probing behind them and understanding the analysis on which they were based. And he lacked either the personnel or the organizational ability to produce such analysis quickly enough to satisfy the working group's accelerating schedule.

Although his specific proposals did not prevail, Allen successfully persuaded his colleagues that outright subsidies for low-income students were essential, and that no scheme relying solely on market rate loans and "low income insurance" would suffice. While the eventual proposals were not nearly so generous as the Commissioner would have liked—nor were they so costly—in a large sense Allen's concern with the plight of the needy student did influence the working group and helped shape the assumptions on which the analytic skills of Butler's office were put to work.

The main constraint the working group had to reckon with in seeking a better allocation of federal student aid funds was the assumption that the budget had no "new money" to apply to this purpose, other than the increases projected for existing programs. Their fiscal 1971 cost was estimated at $633 million and was expected to rise to $806 million the following year.

Since three of the four programs (Opportunity Grants, Work-Study and National Defense Loans) were already fairly well focused on low-income students, the principal budgetary leeway came from reallocating the interest subsidies that the Guaranteed Loan Program afforded to those less needy.[b] HEW data showed that under the present programs, loan subsidies were going to students from families earning as much as $20,000 a year. But ending such benefits raised a political question, for it meant denying aid to hundreds of thousands of middle-income families in order to make more available to the poor.

Although this decision held electoral implications for the administration, it was made with surprisingly little hesitation. Moynihan wryly advised his colleagues that the subsidy cutoff should be set high enough to cover the middle class; "They should be covered," he said, "because the middle class *appreciates* money." But neither he nor anyone else in the working group resisted the proposition that if the total amount were limited, as inevitably it was, it should be directed first to the poorest part of the population and stretched upward only to the point at which the sums that could be guaranteed to the hypothetical family with no income would begin to fall below the level necessary to accomplish the program's goals.

In its way, this decision was bolder than that underlying the administration's Family Assistance Program. For the welfare reform scheme, backstopped by billions of additional dollars, added many families to the ranks of those eligible for aid, but it did not deny benefits to those presently receiving them and would reduce those benefits only in a few states with exceptionally generous welfare policies. The student aid proposals, by contrast, would deny all subsidies to many who could expect to get them under the extant program, and while it would add many potential new recipients, the shift was clearly away from the working- and middle-class population and toward the poor.

[b]Rearranging the subsidy structure of the other three programs would also be necessary, but would not greatly change the target population.

One might have supposed the Nixon administration would move instead to provide some benefits to as many middle-income students as possible, even if doing so meant eliminating the larger subsidies that the Great Society programs had begun to channel to the poor. It would have caused no greater drain on the budget, and it might have won favor for the president among his "silent majority."

But the working group headed in the other direction. To be sure, its members considered the political costs, and chose not to concentrate aid so heavily on the very poor that none would be left for families above the poverty line. But once assured by Butler's analysis that a flexible subsidy structure could be built on projected budget levels in such a way that a cutoff point in the vicinity of $10,000 family income was feasible, there was little hesitation about barring aid to all above that line.

The sums guaranteed to individual students were modest. The "financing floor" was set at $1,300 a year, roughly the amount that a family with ten thousand dollars of income was thought able to apply each year to the college education of one of its children.[c] The government would deliver this entire sum only to families earning less than $4,500, and even for such poverty-stricken students part of the aid would take the form of subsidized loans. Above $4,500, the federal boost would moderate, with outright grants disappearing quickly and loan subsidies also phasing out at ten thousand dollars income.

Only Commissioner Allen was unhappy with that limit, and he conceded that extending aid to more of the middle income population—with a commensurate increase in help for the poorest—would cost substantially more than a simple extension of existing programs. But he stood his ground and in time the president was given the choice between cutoff points at $10,000 or $12,000. The costs of the two alternatives were estimated to diverge (in fiscal 1972) by $400 million, and Nixon picked the lower figure, even though he was advised that meant denying subsidies to about 620,000 additional students who would be eligible at the higher level. Of course, the president was also given the traditional "Option 3," which was to leave existing programs intact and was reminded of the possible political gains from continuing to underwrite interest payments for a large part of "Middle America." But Morgan's decision memorandum was explicit: "The working group recommends Alternative 1 ($10,000), with the exception of Jim Allen who prefers Alternative 2 ($12,000)."[d] No one wanted to retain the existing subsidy structure. All counselled the president to move toward an approach that would guarantee student aid to the neediest, and withhold it from those less impoverished.

---

[c]In 1969-70, tuition, room and board in public colleges averaged about $1200; in private institutions, tuition alone exceeded $1500.

[d]The full text of the higher education working group's "decision memorandum" appears in Appendix C of this volume.

The Career Education Program

The working group wanted to recognize the distinctive role that community colleges were coming to play in American postsecondary education and to highlight their potential for equipping high school graduates with useful job skills. Secretary Finch had been pressing since summer for some federal initiative on behalf of community colleges and "career education." Commissioner Allen was determined to broaden the definition of higher education to embrace such activities and to give an added boost to the burgeoning community college movement. The Labor Department, in the person of Assistant Secretary Rosow, deemed the encouragement of employable skills and relevant education an important element of the kind of postsecondary reform that Washington should promote.

No one on the Morgan group disagreed. In 1969, there were nearly 900 two-year colleges in the United States and more were opening every month. They constituted much the fastest growing sector within the world of nonprofit postsecondary education and already enrolled nearly one out of every five students. An obvious role for the federal government was to provide financial incentives to channel this growth in the direction of "career education" rather than liberal arts. The question was how to do it at a reasonable cost, and in searching for an answer to that question, the working group faced a classic choice. HEW strongly favored—and in this, for once, the Office of Education and the secretary's aides agreed—the creation of a new categorical program of "project grants" to individual colleges, which would approach Washington with proposals outlining their plans.

The Bureau of the Budget, on the other hand, playing its traditional role to the hilt, wanted to consolidate the management of a wide array of existing program authorities, then lodged in diverse parts of HEW, the Labor Department and other agencies, under a single new "targetted staff unit" that would oversee a governmentwide approach to the subject.

Once persuaded that existing program authority alone would not sustain a major presidential initiative in this realm, Nathan further refined his thinking about community colleges along "New Federalism" lines and proposed a program of formula grants to the states—that is, a sort of specialized revenue sharing that would assign to state officials the principal responsibility for deciding which institutions to aid and on what terms. He and his staff vigorously resisted the creation of yet another categorical program that would empower USOE to make project grants.

The Budget Bureau plan also stipulated that federal funds could only be applied to the start-up costs of new programs in occupational fields that the Secretary of Labor held to be in short supply and that the states would have to match Washington's money. It was to be an incentive program, not a subsidy for routine operating costs.

As the weeks passed, the entire working group came to favor Nathan's strategy. More precisely, it got so caught up in other contentious issues that it had little time for the details of a relatively small program the basic concept of which everyone liked. Eventually, even the HEW representatives agreed to the Budget Bureau scheme. Hence although the president's decision memorandum contained both options, the Morgan group pronounced itself unanimously in favor of the formula grant approach.

The National Foundation for Higher Education

With the basic shape of the student aid package determined, with a sort of gentlemanly decision to "agree to disagree" on cutoff points and funding levels, and with no serious dispute over community colleges and occupational education, the working group next turned to a quartet of complex and controversial issues that were far from resolution: What to do about the crisis in financing higher education that had led to enormous pressure for direct federal aid to colleges and universities? How to incorporate in presidential policy the notion that Washington ought to foster postsecondary reform and innovation? How to respond to the perceived "loss of excellence" in major research universities that Moynihan, DuBridge, and some of their academic colleagues deemed an acute and worsening problem in need of a national solution? And, more generally, how to accomplish these varied objectives while strengthening the autonomy of higher education and keeping government out of its internal affairs?

The working group had neither the leisure nor the budgetary slack to devise specialized responses to such distinctive concerns, and there was no time or will to scan the entire federal establishment with an eye to harmonizing the approaches of a dozen agencies. Somehow, a relatively uncomplicated unifying idea or structure had to be found.

In this quest, the working group had also to contend with a number of narrower issues. The nation's traditionally black colleges and universities were financially distressed and looked to Washington for specialized assistance. Allen, Finch, and Moynihan were all sensitive to their plight and troubled by the charge that the Nixon administration was unconcerned about it. None of their colleagues disagreed. Indeed, giving some sort of federal boost to black colleges had been taken for granted ever since the president's upbeat response to the Finch-Moynihan memorandum in October. The question was how to do so in a manner that would be helpful without taking excessive political or Constitutional risks and without greatly increased expenditures.

The working group also faced the question of whether to propose an executive branch reorganization designed to elevate the status of higher education. The idea of a separate Department of Education had been around for decades, and bills to create one had regularly been filed in Congress, but

Counselor Moynihan had a different notion. Reasoning that a Department of Education would inevitably be dominated by the interests of elementary and secondary schools, that the policy concerns of colleges and universities were different from those of the public schools and unlikely to be well understood by the former superintendents who tended to become commissioners of education, and that higher education was deeply engaged in scientific research as well as student instruction, in December he had urged Nixon to propose the establishment of a Department of Higher Education and Research. It would consolidate the postsecondary functions of USOE, together with the National Institutes of Health, the National Science Foundation, and diverse other research authorities ranging from NASA to the Atomic Energy Commission. Moynihan argued that "higher education . . . desperately needs coherent national support, guided by national priorities" and that the government ought "to distribute the large amounts of money we routinely spend in a manner that adds up to policy." Although others in the administration were anything but enamored of this particular approach to reorganization—when he learned of it, Commissioner Allen, who wanted a full-fledged Department of Education, wrote the President that he had "the strongest professional and personal feelings" about the matter—the notion of an agency attuned to higher education persisted. It had a forceful advocate in Moynihan, whose basic points were hard to fault: Absent a separate higher education unit of some sort, no one in the executive branch had the responsibility for thinking of higher education as a whole. Absent a unified focus for its activities, higher education would either exploit the federal budget (by going from one agency to the next with its shopping list and never adding up the total) or be victimized by transient governmental enthusiasms that ignored the peculiarities of the industry. And without a generalized agency of this sort, the higher education community never had to put its own federal house in order, fix its priorities or thrash out its differences.

Another consideration for the working group, persistently raised by the Budget Bureau, was curbing the proliferation of categorical programs in the field of higher education. Over the years a number had been enacted. Some had never been funded. Others, such as Foreign Language and Area Studies, while vibrant were small, limited in their appeal, and hardly deserving of the specialized bureaucracies set up to run them. Still others, such as graduate training fellowships, persisted even though, in view of the growing surplus of college teachers, their funds might better be used elsewhere. The challenge was to mold a number of these legislative authorities into a single, flexible format that could adapt itself to changing social and educational needs, that would discourage the enactment of still more categorical programs, and that could be smoothly administered by one large agency instead of diverse small bureaus.

In addition to these sizable concerns, working group members kept peppering each other with miscellaneous proposals, some of their own devising, others borrowed from elsewhere. DuBridge suggested a new program of federal "merit scholarships" for college students. Butler, Allen, and Rosow had separate versions of a federally financed "higher education reform" program. The Hester Task Force had recommended the formation of a National Academy of Higher Education, modeled on the National Academy of Sciences, to conduct policy studies and to advise the government.

With the student aid proposals destined to consume most of whatever additional budget authority would be available for higher education and with little time or inclination to dwell on each of these scattered proposals and concerns, the working group needed a unifying concept.

It arrived, *deus ex Moynihan*, in the first week of February, when the presidential advisor seized upon a recent Carnegie Commission recommendation and pressed it upon his colleagues in somewhat changed form as a National Foundation for Higher Education.[17] A new agency, outside of HEW, akin to the National Science Foundation, but not a cabinet department with large operating responsibilities, the proposed foundation quickly became a structural solution to many distinct policy problems.

The foundation idea had several evident virtues. First, it was a *large* idea, something worthy of a presidential initiative. The nascent Message to Congress clearly needed another such element. Second, because it built upon a proposal of the Carnegie Commission, it might be presumed—so the working group allowed itself to think—that it would find favor in the eyes of influential educators. Third, it was a vehicle for bringing at least a modest amount of resources to bear on higher education *per se* without snaring Washington in more categorical traps.

A predictable split within the working group appeared early in discussions of the foundation idea. Butler and Allen saw little merit in a scheme that would strip their department of its primacy in the field of higher education, that would reduce the Office of Education (insofar as it retained any postsecondary responsibilities) to the role of a check-writing agency, and that would scrap a number of familiar HEW programs and authorities. Others in the working group, however, feeling that HEW was ill equipped to handle higher education policy issues with sensitivity and ill organized to give the subject enough top-level attention, favored the proposal in part *because* it would force such a division of responsibility.

But the dispute over turf was temporarily eclipsed by another elementary group dynamic that the foundation proposal responded to: It permitted consensus by sponging up a great many new and not-so-new ideas. One account has termed it a "garbage can for old programs,"[18] and as the idea took shape, it certainly did provide a way of satisfying the Budget Bureau's yen to consolidate a number of narrower endeavors into a single entity. But what was insidiously tempting about the foundation proposal was that every member of the working group could see in it a solution to his own favorite problem, a vehicle for his fondest idea. The implicit contradictions stayed beneath the surface.

Empowered to expend its funds on practically anything under the broad heading of "excellence, innovation, and reform," its flexibility would enable it to swallow a number of extant program authorities and to decide whether to devote resources to them or to wholly different activities and to change its focus as the needs and concerns of higher education itself changed. It could channel aid to black colleges, or to visionary curriculum reform schemes. It could even provide some temporary institutional support to hard-pressed universities. But none of these would be permanent obligations and leaving the choices to a foundation board drawn from the higher education community meant that advocates of a particular cause would have to persuade a jury of their peers. Hence the pressure on elected officials to find a federal solution to every higher education problem would abate.

The idea gained force as Moynihan advanced his version of what was to become the philosophical underpinning of the entire message, with its stress on the need "for the federal government to help academic communities to pursue excellence and reform in fields of their own choosing . . . and by means of their own choice."[e] The president would, in essence, first restate his year-old position on the need for higher education to set its own house in order, and then volunteer federal funds to help it do so.

Thus a sort of symbiosis appeared between the working group's need to respond to a number of half-related issues and the presumed desirability of giving American higher education a structure and resources to address its own needs without too heavy a federal hand. The National Foundation could serve both purposes.

Yet a tension also remained between the two, and the message would show it. The goals of flexibility and autonomy demanded that the foundation not be overloaded with specific purposes. But the impulse to respond to numerous concerns of and about higher education called, at the very least, for some pointed hints that the administration recognized these as problems and expected the foundation to resolve them. The eventual compromise was a generalized statement of purpose for the foundation, combined with a string of carefully chosen examples of concerns that *could* be addressed within those purposes. In time, virtually every one of the special enthusiasms of the working group members was somehow tied onto the foundation and cited in the message as an illustration of the activities the new agency might support. There was even a hint of institutional aid; not explicit formula payments to every college, but tucked away in the foundation's mandate "to strengthen colleges and universities or courses of instruction that play a uniquely valuable role in American higher education or that are faced with special difficulties." That was vague enough to embrace Tougaloo along with Stanford, but it was clearly aimed at institutions wanting federal aid, and the essence of the foundation was that its outlays would

eThe full text of Richard M. Nixon's "Special Message to the Congress on Higher Education," March 19, 1970, appears in Appendix B of this volume. Throughout this chapter, all presidential quotations are from this message unless otherwise indicated.

go directly to colleges and universities *qua* institutions, whereas the other key elements of the emerging policy package were intended for needy students or for the states.

Most members of the working group were prepared to overlook the latent conflicts among the foundation's diverse missions and the fact that too many of them were being saddled onto an infant agency with none-too-large a budget. The hour was late, the participants were weary, and no one wanted to challenge the validity of a colleague's idea. Even—perhaps especially—at the level of presidential policy, time is the ultimate decisionmaker, and some advisors play the clock better than others. Besides, each idea had merit, and it was easier to embrace them all within the foundation—and leave it to the "higher education community" to decide which should come first—than to select among them.

In late February, Moynihan listed eleven purposes that the foundation was to be "authorized and directed" to achieve; these ranged from international scholarly exchange programs to the support of social science research, the encouragement of minority group enrollments and the formulation of national higher education policy. It was overly ambitious, to say the least, but it was certainly tempting. So much so that Moynihan and most of his working group colleagues failed to draw a lesson from his own reflections on the mid-sixties Community Action Program, of which he had written: "The essential problem . . . was that the one term concealed at least four quite distinct meanings. . . . The task of government, in this case of the President's advisors, was first to discern these four different meanings, to make sure they were understood by those who had to make decisions about them, and to keep all concerned alert to the dangers of not keeping the distinctions clearly enough in mind."[19]

In part because his eye was uncommonly clear and in part because his own agency stood to lose the most, Lewis Butler dissented once again. In early March, two weeks before the message was to be sent to Capitol Hill, he memorialized his colleagues in stern words: "The proposed Foundation for Higher Education is a superficially appealing idea which, when analyzed—at least by me—turns into mush." "What," he asked rhetorically, "is to be the mission of the Foundation?" and then mooted an answer: "All things to all men?" He insisted that the working group recognize the "fundamental differences among us" and the folly of "turning them all over to a Foundation and abdicating to that institution these decisions on Federal policy." Such an agency, he felt, "cannot do all of these things. . . . Some members of our group are going to be disappointed." Worse, he argued, the proposal smacked "of the past federal practice, of which we have been as a new Administration, so critical, of creating a new institution when we don't know what else to do." He continued for three single-spaced pages: If the Foundation were as free of political pressure as its advocates claimed, it would not be accountable to the president. If quasi-independent agencies are a desirable format for national social policy, "why not a Poverty Foundation instead of OEO . . . a Health Foundation, an Environmental Foundation?" How was the foundation to be a powerful engine for the reform of higher education if its governing board was to be selected from, and presumably representative of, the diverse interests of the higher education establishment? Why, if education is a continuous process, carve the federal leadership role among additional unconnected agencies?

It was a strong assault, but it did not go unrebuffed. Moynihan responded with a powerful restatement of reasons why the toughest postsecondary policy challenges confronting the federal government—the maintenance of excellence, the encouragement of reform, and the succor of Negro colleges—"are not suited to the normal administrative procedures of a hierarchical bureaucracy." "To the contrary," he asserted, "most of them can only be made as collegial decisions, in which the communities that will be benefited or slighted participate in the choices." Finally, he summed up, "There is one basic political argument on behalf of a National Foundation for Higher Education. The President needs to put forward a proposal in the field of education which is distinctive, which can be identified with him, and which proposes that a reasonably large sum of money be spent."

HEW's tactical dilemma was that it had nothing to substitute for the foundation. A small program of project grants aimed at innovation, yes, but nothing that addressed the other concerns of the working group. Moreover, the department's objections to the National Foundation idea could be read as a campaign to preserve its turf and its primacy in a policy arena that the foundation, once created, would surely dominate.

Yet Butler's and Allen's protests were not dismissed, nor did the working group simply override them. Absent consensus, it was a decision for the president to make, and it was put to him in the "decision memorandum" that he received a week before the message was to be sent. The idea was outlined; six "pro" and five "con" arguments were spelled out. And the "recommendation" section was straightforward: "The working group is divided over the Foundation, but has no good alternative to propose. Dr. Moynihan, Dr. DuBridge and Mr. Rosow strongly favor the Foundation. Mr. Stein and Mr. Nathan are, on balance, disposed toward it. Mr. Butler and Commissioner Allen object to the Foundation, as does Secretary Finch. . . ." Morgan reserved his own views for a separate cover memo, but his colleagues had the impression that his respect for Moynihan's judgment and his distaste for the Office of Education led him also to urge the president to endorse the new agency.

Philosophy and Rhetoric

The working group's gradual conversion to the National Foundation proposal was coupled with ratification of the basic ideas on which it rested, which were essentially Moynihan's conception of the proper federal role in American higher education. As sketched in a memorandum to his colleagues, these began with the proposition that "We must, above all, provide a general statement of the appropriate Federal relationship to higher education." He observed that it was a "vastly complex subject that 'just growed'. So many Federal agencies are involved with colleges and universities, under so many different laws and with so many different purposes, that we are long overdue for a clear statement of the *philosophy* that underlies that relationship. No one has done it, and it would be completely consistent with the reform emphasis of this Administration."

Introducing policy where previously there had only been programs mattered greatly to the presidential advisor.[f] He had written that over the years "the structure of American government, and the pragmatic tradition of American politics, too much defined public policy in forms of program, and in consequence has inhibited the development of true policy."[20] Higher education, he insisted to his working group colleagues, afforded a splendid opportunity to make sense out of a welter of federal programs by recasting them around a coherent and purposeful set of policies.

He proposed to root those policies in two themes: opportunity for students to attend college without regard to their economic condition and a noninterventionist federal stance toward higher education institutions that did not let Washington's dollars get too much in the way of academic self-determination. One passage in the president's message would evoke that idea in the assertion that "it is past time the Federal Government acknowledged its own responsibility for bringing about, through the forms of support it has given and the conditions of that support, a serious distortion of the activities of our centers of academic excellence." Such distortions would be immeasurably worsened, Moynihan argued, if the tendency to punish colleges for student disruptions were allowed to become a pillar of federal policy, and he took satisfaction from his success a year earlier in persuading Nixon to reject such tactics. But the congressional impulse to punish disorderly undergraduates was only the most recent instance of a long-lived and more fundamental concern, namely that Washington and the universities were both getting too accustomed to a buyer-seller relationship in which the vendor provided whatever the purchaser wanted and the buyer gradually began to shape the seller's activities. This, Moynihan believed, would in time prove damaging both to the higher education system and to the larger society. Not even the university leadership, he

---

[f]In an essay that had commanded much attention in the early days of the administration, Moynihan argued for and began to outline a "national urban policy." A year later, favoring Wilbur Mills—whose Ways and Means Committee was then considering the Family Assistance Plan—with a visit to the chairman's alma mater, he would address the subject of "Policy vs. Program in the 1970s." See "Toward a National Urban Policy," Chapter 1 in Daniel P. Moynihan, ed., *Toward a National Urban Policy* (New York: Basic Books, 1970); and "Policy vs. Program in the 1970s," Chapter 15 in Moynihan, *Coping: Essays on the Practice of Government* (New York: Random House, 1973).

suspected, was fully cognizant of this threat. Beset with campus concerns and hungering after the federal dollar, too many college presidents and their Washington lobbyists were so lost in program particulars that they could ill comprehend the ecological changes in their environment.

This carefully delineated philosophy was not, one may suppose, something the president expected to find himself articulating although in a large sense it was fully consistent with the New Federalism's pattern of sorting out governmental functions and withdrawing Washington from activities it was ill equipped to manage well.

Most of the men sitting around Ed Morgan's conference table thought this stance made sense. These were Republican ideas, conservative ideas, but in a realm where federal intrusions are viewed by most liberals as evil, they were also progressive ideas. They resonated of academic freedom and collegiate self-government. They built a conceptual base capable of sustaining however large or small an edifice the budget would permit, and one perhaps especially worth building at a time when the structure atop it was not going to scrape the clouds.

Moynihan's image of a National Foundation for Higher Education was essentially neutral with respect to funding levels. He assumed that the monies devoted by the national government to higher education would continue to increase and wanted to ensure that they did so against a policy backdrop that would keep them from making mischief. But the self-restraint he urged on Washington was also singularly well-suited to a time of budgetary stringency.

One of the paradoxes of reform—and most everyone concerned with the administration's domestic policy making in those days was satisfied that reform was the hallmark of the Nixon era—is that in the absence of additional money it may resemble retrenchment. Efforts to redirect programs so as to make more effective use of existing sums typically mean that some who enjoyed a share of that money under the previous arrangements will lose those benefits in order that others may receive them. And it was the particular fate of the Nixon administration to follow two presidencies that had encouraged enormous growth of the federal domestic role in ways that led the nation to associate federally sponsored reform with handsome sums serving as virtual bribes to the affected clienteles to change their ways.

James E. Allen, Jr., had not abandoned that linkage. The commissioner was increasingly uneasy with the new administration's coupling of reform with a cramped approach to federal spending. He had to live with the acrimony that followed Nixon's two successive vetoes of education appropriations, and he was reluctant to let the president's—and his own—maiden statements of national education policy be marketed with a bargain basement pricetag.

In a blunt memorandum sent to the president a scant three days before the higher education message went to Congress (a memo which, to my knowledge, Nixon was never shown), Allen all but pleaded for a different approach: "We are now at another crossroads point for American education," he asserted, "much like that at the beginning of this century when the Nation chose to commit itself to providing a free public secondary education for all. It is an historic point—one where strong leadership can take advantage of the new needs and of the unrest and dissatisfaction to effect changes that will truly revitalize and modernize higher education." The leadership he sought was nothing less than "a new appraisal of the extent of public responsibility for and investment in higher education." The Message to Congress then in near-final form was, he felt, "at best . . . an interim kind of statement within existing fiscal constraints, and we can hope for any kind of positive reaction only if it is presented as such."

Billing the message as interim and constrained, however, was the farthest thing from the minds of Daniel P. Moynihan and most of his working group colleagues. They saw it, to the contrary, as a durable philosophic statement that transcended both budget limitations and programmatic content. It was nothing less than a basic charter—as no previous presidential Message to Congress had ever been devoted wholly to higher education issues, it was legitimately a sort of charter—setting forth the proper relationship between the national government and that important national enterprise known as higher education. Even if its substantive proposals had carried not a nickel of federal funds, it was a document that would stand in its own right.

Perhaps no one but Moynihan actually entertained quite such an ambitious conception, for probably no one else involved with its preparation had such high regard for the authority of a presidential message as a statement of national direction or for its paragraphs as a sophisticated public policy art form. But the others believed, or let themselves be persuaded, that it was more consequential than Allen thought and that the richness of the policy formulation would, if nothing else, help to compensate for the fact that its programs were somewhat less filling than their consumers might wish.

Little remained except to harmonize the substantive proposals and the philosophical themes into a final document ready for the president's signature. That entailed two steps: a series of presidential decisions on specific program options and funding levels, and final agreement on the wording of the message.

The first was Morgan's responsibility and, characteristic of the orderly methods of John Ehrlichman's early domestic policy regime, it meant drafting a "decision memorandum" for the president to consider. Into a slender notebook went a three-page summary and six "tabs" covering more detailed exegeses of individual items. Four questions called for substantive choices, and a series of budget options was keyed to each of the program decisions. Under each heading, there was a capsule description of existing programs, a discussion of problems and issues, a sketch of the working group's alternatives, the pros and cons of each, and a statement of working group recommendations. It was an orderly, workmanlike, and, as far as it went, neutral recapitulation of months of deliberations. What it did not do, of course, was raise issues or present programs that the working group had rejected out of hand. There was, for example, no discussion of general aid to universities, of a special initiative exclusively for black colleges, or of a national educational opportunity bank. These and numerous other ideas, large and small, had not made it through the working group filter and consequently they did not appear among the president's choices.

Presidential language was the responsibility of the White House speech-writing staff, whose members were assigned to topics in a somewhat arbitrary manner. It happened that William Safire found himself entrusted with the higher education verbiage, as he had been a few weeks previously with elementary and secondary. But the experience of the earlier message had taught Morgan and his colleagues two lessons. Speechwriters who are brought into the deliberations before substantive content has been settled tend to want to insert their own programs as well as their phrases. And messages that go through too many drafts over too long a period are a misery for all concerned.

Partly for those reasons and partly because the hour was so late when the president's final decisions were relayed back to the working group, Safire did not embark on his first draft until mid-March. The Allen-Finn language of late December had long since been forgotten, although a number of its ideas had survived, and some of them resurfaced in the draft that Morgan had me write—as a sort of starting place for Safire—on March fifteenth. Safire in turn drew on a few of my paragraphs and built heavily on Moynihan's conceptual foundation as he readied his first official draft which was delivered for review just three days before it was scheduled to reach Congress. The working group members hastily scanned it, fed in their factual corrections and stylistic suggestions, and Safire had a semi-final version ready the following day.

Meanwhile, other offices in the White House and HEW began to crank out fact sheets, supplementary explanations, mass mailings, and large charts suitable for press briefings.

All seemed to be in order for a presidential message to move from the White House to Capitol Hill, but a last minute flareup in the Budget Bureau caused the deletion of some dollar figures from the document on the very morning it was sent. It appeared that some of Nathan's colleagues for the first time got around to tallying the costs of the various higher education initiatives, and they reacted badly to the totals. It was simply too late to renegotiate substantive matters, so a few numbers were dropped for later consideration. For example, the last Safire draft included a spending projection for the student aid package—$800 million in fiscal 1972—that the working group estimated to be the amount necessary to carry out the program along the agreed-upon policy lines. Nathan thought he had secured the necessary approvals, but in the final hours Budget Director Mayo refused to commit the administration to that specific dollar total for a fiscal year that would not even commence until sixteen months later, so out it came.

All else went according to plan on March nineteenth. The president videotaped some remarks for later use on television. In them, he highlighted the student aid provisions—"Under the plan I proposing today, no qualified student who wants to go to college would be barred from doing so by the lack of money." He noted that "it would not be a free ride" but "the important thing is you could afford to go to college." He also spoke warmly of the National Foundation. It took two minutes.

The press briefing in the White House Roosevelt Room was handled by Moynihan, Allen, and Butler, with a Budget Bureau economic specialist coming in to explain the more abstruse consequences of the National Student Loan Association.

Allen led off. In keeping with his desire not to overstate the significance of the proposals, he termed the message a "highly important first step." He outlined the student aid proposals, and the Career Education program, then Moynihan explained the National Foundation.

Reflecting the tenor of the times, the first question from a reporter asked whether "any part of this proposed Act [would] be directed towards campus unrest?" Reflecting the general press inclination to emphasize dollars, the next batch of queries concerned proposed funding levels for the several programs. The discussion grew somewhat involved, befitting the intricacy of the subject, but was generally amiable. After half an hour, one newsman gave the pro forma "Thank you," and it was over. About the same time, a White House messenger deposited the requisite pair of signed typescripts in the appropriate House and Senate offices, and the message had become an official communication from the president to the Congress of the United States. The Nixon administration now had an education policy.

Appraising the Nixon Legacy

The Immediate Response

The first half of 1970 was an inauspicious time for the president's proposals to get the reception their authors felt they deserved.

On January 26, Nixon went on nationwide television to veto the Labor-HEW-OEO appropriations bill. Although he insisted that "The increased spending ordered by Congress for the most part simply provides more dollars for the same old programs without making the urgent new reforms that are needed," not everyone in his audience was persuaded by the president's statement that his veto was "in the long-range interests of better education."

On February 17, Leon Panetta, Director of HEW's Office of Civil Rights, was sacked for excessive zeal in desegregating the nation's schools.

On April 8, the Senate refused to confirm G. Harrold Carswell, the southern judge Nixon had nominated to fill the "Brandeis chair" on the U.S. Supreme Court when his first candidate, Clement F. Haynsworth, Jr., was rejected. The next day, the president voiced anger and despair over his inability to put a southerner and a strict constructionist onto the high court.

On April 13, signing the "elementary and secondary education amendments of 1969," he said he was doing so with "considerable reluctance."

On April 21, testifying on the administration's plan to provide federal aid to "racially impacted areas," sociologist James Coleman, whose work had figured so prominently in White House policy councils, asserted that such money "would not be wisely spent."[1]

On April 28, Vice President Spiro Agnew called for an end to "the era of appeasement" on campus, for "immediate expulsion" of disruptive students, and for the ouster of Yale President Kingman Brewster.

On April 30, the president was back on television to inform the nation that he had ordered troops into Cambodia.

On May 1, during a visit to the Pentagon, Nixon was heard to speak of "those bums . . . blowing up the campuses."

On May 4, four Kent State University students were killed by the bullets of the Ohio National Guard.

On May 6, Interior Secretary Walter Hickel's celebrated letter protesting Nixon's isolation and the administration's alienation of young people became public.

On May 9, 75,000 antiwar demonstrators massed in the nation's capital.

On May 14, two students were killed by police bullets at Jackson State College.

On June 3, speaking at West Point, the vice president again condemned student radicals and "criminal misfits."

On June 10, Education Commissioner James Allen was dismissed in consequence of his dissent from administration policies regarding school desegregation and the Indo-China war.

Relations between the White House and the nation's education community were at an historic low, and relations between the two ends of Pennsylvania Avenue were little better. It is not surprising that the reception accorded the president's substantive proposals was chilly, and it is correspondingly difficult to tell how much of that reception was based on their specific content and how much on the general climate.

"There is hardly a platitude ever uttered about education," began *The Washington Post*, "that is not contained in the President's special Message to Congress on educational reform." Its proposals, insisted the editorialist, were "a political ploy, a stall, an evasion." *The New Republic* termed it a "mousy document." *The New York Times* analogized it to "a pledge to a drowning man that help will come as soon as the experts find out why he is swimming so poorly." The Johnson administration's respected education staffer, Douglass Cater, welcomed the proposal for a National Institute of Education but decried the decision to delay additional financial commitment until there is proof of "more education for the dollar." American Federation of Teachers president David Selden called on Commissioner Allen to resign as a "signal to everyone interested in public education that the Nixon proposals are inadequate, deceptive and injurious to the children of this country." Allen, it soon developed, did not need Selden's advice. Ironically, it was Joseph Alsop, whose hawkishness on Vietnam made him one of the few pundits to support Nixon's foreign policy, who observed that the education reform message "may just possibly turn out to be his most important state paper to date."[2]

On the afternoon it was delivered, the higher education message was roundly denounced by the American Council on Education and most of the other major Washington-based university groups as a "severely constrained proposal."[3] The administration's emphasis on loans as the principal student aid vehicle for all but the neediest, its redirection of subsidies from the middle class to the poor, its failure to include an institutional assistance program, and its eagerness to scrap a number of familiar authorizations were the chief complaints. Underlying them were two more general discontents: the president's overall budget strictures with respect to higher education at a time when many colleges faced deficits and the fact that the administration's policy package had been assembled with little input from the affected constituency.

As the weeks passed, HEW officials held background discussions with education associations, the president met with a group of university presidents, hands were held, viewpoints heard, clarifications offered, and slowly a grudging, partial turnaround was noticeable. No educator could easily oppose the notion that poverty-stricken students should be helped to attend college or dispute the proposition that universities should function with the least possible federal interference, and not many were prepared to argue that loans should be hard to come by. So in a few private letters, public statements, and occasional congressional testimony, some support was voiced for the principles underlying the president's program, although such endorsements were usually followed by a lengthy list of objections to particular features of the actual proposals. Two Brookings scholars termed the administration package "bold reform on an inadequate budget."[4] It is likely that for those on the campuses—who generally form their impressions of such events from the mailings of their Washington representatives—the inadequacies of the budget eclipsed the boldness of the reform, particularly since many of the programs marked for change were popular and familiar, while the proposed replacements were vague and uncertain.

The congressional response was almost as cool. Not even the Republicans, who customarily introduce bills on behalf of a president of their party, were enthusiastic about the administration's initiatives. Senator Javits and Representative Quie dropped the bill into the hoppers as a courtesy, but promptly submitted their own higher education proposals as well, and signalled that they felt no obligation to lobby intensively on behalf of the White House legislation. The response by the Democratic majority ranged from apathy to outrage.[5]

Yet twenty-seven months later, Richard Nixon was to sign an act of Congress—the Education Amendments of 1972—that embodied many of the proposals he had made in March, 1970.[a] He was to do so with almost no fanfare, save for bitter comments on Congress' failure to deal sternly enough with court-ordered busing. He took scant credit for the ideas in the legislation, nor for the philosophy underlying them. Counselor Moynihan, by then long since returned to academe, was startled in the summer of 1972 to be presented by the president with the pen used a few weeks earlier to sign the historic amendments and afterwards wrote of the "private" signing that "It was almost as if the administration had sought to conceal the act."[6]

It is no small task to trace responsibility for the specific provisions of complex legislation, and historians will scrutinize the 1972 Amendments for years to come. It would be irresponsible to assert that the provisions resembling the administration's proposals emerged from Congress because Richard Nixon had suggested them. That the Democrats controlled both chambers during the entire period is itself ample reason to think otherwise. It is far more likely that

[a]Alone among the president's major proposals, the Commission on School Finance required no action by Congress. Created by Executive Order 11513 on March 3, 1970, and fully constituted in June 1970 under the chairmanship of Neil H. McElroy, it worked hard, sponsored a number of research studies, and delivered its final report in 1972. See President's Commission on School Finance, *Schools, People and Money: The Need for Educational Reform*, Final Report, Washington, D.C., 1972.

in the subtle ways by which public policies grow to maturity in American society and in the impalpable processes by which consensus is reached, these were simply ideas that had ripened and were ready to be plucked.

Nevertheless, the correlation remains surprisingly high between the policy recommendations of a conservative Republican president and the key elements in a far-reaching bill enacted by a moderately liberal Democratic Congress. While the possibility must be acknowledged that the same legislation would have ended up on Nixon's desk even if the White House had never proposed anything, the fact is that the omnibus act the president signed embodied enough of the ideas he had espoused that he could reasonably have seized the opportunity to share in the credit for it.

That he did not is indicative of many things, of which perhaps the most important is that March 1970 was the zenith of the Nixon White House's interest in the substance of education policy. By Christmas, Moynihan was packing to return to Harvard. In August 1970, Science Advisor DuBridge had retired to California. His replacement, Dr. Edward E. David, Jr., was a distinguished scientist, but was also the first presidential science advisor not drawn directly from the academy. Although HEW Secretary Finch had come to the White House as a presidential counselor and although Edward L. Morgan retained nominal responsibility within the Ehrlichman staff for education policy, there was simply no one in the vicinity of the Oval Office who combined an interest in education with knowledge of the subject matter and access to the president.

While the White House staff was losing horsepower in the field of education, the Department of HEW was growing stronger. Allen's successor as commissioner, Sidney P. Marland, Jr., and new HEW Secretary Elliot L. Richardson were more commanding individuals than the men they replaced and were determined to retrieve the initiative in policy deliberations affecting matters within their domains.

The only area where the White House kept the reins tight was school desegregation, which consumed more and more of Morgan's time between 1970 and the presidential election two years later. It was the one aspect of education with high visibility and great political sensitivity, and Morgan was effectively made czar over all administration policies, actions, and statements touching on the subject. Among other things, this left him scant time to devote to the progress of other education programs and legislation.

Moreover, the president had apparently lost whatever appetite he may have had for education policy. He had offered up his program. No one seemed interested in embracing it. He evidently decided there was more mileage to be gotten from opposing large expenditures on social programs such as education than from proposing new ones.[b] And the rupture between his administration and the nation's education community seemed inoperable.

---

[b]It may be noted, however, that Nixon's second veto of an education appropriation—in August 1970 for the fiscal year 1971—was overridden by Congress.

The 1970 election campaign scarcely helped. Much of its content, whether voiced by the president or by his mouthpiece, the vice president, was a call for law and order that used campus violence and disruptive students as symbols of the worst in the society. This was not a tactic calculated to endear the administration to the liberal community generally or to educators in particular, nor was it so intended.

The president may have felt betrayed by, and bitter toward, education leaders, and they in turn believed their problems were exacerbated by him. On two different occasions in 1970, people he appointed to look into campus unrest and student alienation weighed in with reports critical of him and his administration. In late July, special advisors Alexander Heard and James Cheek, invited to the White House in the tumultuous aftermath of Cambodia to advise the president on what should be done, came forth with lengthy memoranda which, in the words of one senior presidential aide, started from "the premise that the failures of the national government are the source of campus disorder." Nixon called this stance "very shortsighted."[7]

In late September there appeared the report of the President's Commission on Campus Unrest, known after its chairman as the Scranton Commission. In words evocative of the Kerner Commission a few years earlier, it proclaimed that the nation was splitting in half, with a "new culture" of students faced by an ever less tolerant older society. While unwavering in its condemnation of violence of every stripe, the commission's recommendations appeared to start from the same premise as those of Heard and Cheek: that the solution to the problems of the day lay with the federal government and, in particular, with the President of the United States.[8]

Agnew condemned the Scranton Report as "scapegoating of the most irresponsible sort."[9] The president remained officially silent until several weeks after the election, whereupon he released a length response in the form of a letter to Chairman Scranton. While thanking the commission members for their investment of "time and energy," he insisted that "moral authority . . . does not reside in the Presidency alone" and indicated that the portions of the report implying that it did were less than welcome. He asserted that the vice president deserved plaudits for "unequivocally condemning violence and disruption," and he rejected any suggestion that the commission's views were widely shared by the nation.[10]

Yet as the gap widened between the White House and the education community, a principle was being preserved which, while it did not incline the president to a more activist stance toward education, was nevertheless consistent with the philosophy his higher education message expressed. The academy had to take responsibility for itself, and should not look to Washington to solve its problems or ease its discontents.

This was a double-edged doctrine. It allowed the president to shrug off the insistence that campus woes were the administration's doing and that presidential moral leadership, an altered foreign policy, and a few more billions of dollars were the way to restore order and contentment to academe. But it also said to congressmen and legislators that new criminal penalties, the withdrawal of funds, and other governmental approaches to the highly charged issue of campus unrest were not the proper approach, either, and that precisely because academic freedom was the responsibility of the academy, it should not be imperilled by intrusive political acts. As his higher education message of March 19, 1970, had asserted, "to intervene to impose freedom, is by definition to suppress it."

In all of this there seemed little room for discussions of possible refinements in student aid legislation, just as in the realm of elementary and secondary education it was hard to shift from such volatile issues as busing and appropriations back to a proposal for more and better research. In a highly charged atmosphere, the more political aspects of federal education policy were bound to command attention and to eclipse the less arresting, if more durable, substantive issues such as funding formulae and the structure of new agencies.

The Second Round

Yet legislation was expiring, the president had offered his views on what should replace it, and even if no one at the White House greatly cared about the substance of education policy any more, the administration could not ignore the subject. Little happened on Capitol Hill in 1970, other than some inconclusive hearings, but 1971 brought a new Congress and a fresh legislative cycle, and in the early months of that year the White House restated its education program. This took the form of three more Messages to Congress:

On January 26, 1971, in a catch-all document accompanying the resubmission of various proposals that the 91st Congress had not acted on, Nixon again called for the creation of a National Institute of Education and for the passage of the Emergency School Aid Act to "encourage and to expedite desegregation." Again unmentioned was the latent clash between a research agency said to be needed because ignorance about the educational process doomed worthy compensatory efforts and the establishment of a sizable new spending program that was largely compensatory in nature.

On February 22, the president signed a Message to Congress on higher education. Unlike the one in 1970, which was prepared at the White House, this version was mostly the work of Elliot Richardson's HEW. Shorter than its predecessor and less philosophical in tone, the 1971 message outlined the provisions of two administration bills that accompanied it. The first of these was essentially a reiteration of the student aid provisions that the Morgan working group had developed. A few modifications were incorporated (evidence of Richardson's desire to respond where he could to the desires of the higher education community), but the basic thrust—subsidies for the poor and no institutional aid for the colleges—was the same. The second bill, however, revealed a coup by HEW, for the version of a National Foundation for Higher Education that the administration proferred this time lacked two of the key features that Moynihan had persuaded the working group were essential, but that HEW had never liked: No longer was the foundation to be a freestanding agency akin to the National Science Foundation, but rather an arm of HEW. And where the 1970 message spoke of "excellence, innovation and reform," the 1971 bill linked the foundation only to innovation and reform. Excellence vanished as a stated goal.

HEW executives had naturally objected to the view that the new higher education foundation should be an autonomous agency outside their domain and in the absence of strong figures in the Executive Office of the President willing to press the case for such independence, it followed from Richardson's domination of the policy-making process that the idea would be recaptured by his big department. As for excellence, the word smelled of elitism, stodginess, and ivied walls, whereas the upper echelons of HEW were much taken with the recent report of the Newman Committee with its stress on openness, reform, and experimentation in higher education. Indeed, the 1971 version of the National Foundation may fairly be described as an institutional embodiment of many of the Newman group's ideas, to be carried out within the agency that had spawned that committee and employed several of its members.[11]

On April 6, in the third of these messages, the president urged on Congress a sweeping new program of Special Revenue Sharing for education. Consistent with the administration's doctrine of the New Federalism, this plan—which had counterparts in five other policy domains—complemented the proposal for General Revenue Sharing that would become law in 1972. It would take project grant funds from several large education programs at the elementary and secondary level and convert them into bloc grants that the states and localities could use as they liked within the loose confines of broad national goals.

Education Revenue Sharing was to go nowhere in Congress, but many of the proposals in the other two messages would emerge as law, albeit in modified form.

Chairman John Brademas of the House Subcommittee on Select Education, one of Congress' few education specialists, became persuaded that a National Institute of Education was a worthy idea. He held a lengthy series of sympathetic hearings in 1971. Fittingly, the first witness was Harvard Professor Daniel P. Moynihan. By this time, HEW had contracted with the RAND Corporation for a survey of educational research and a set of blueprints for the proposed institute, so the Congress was able to consider a well-developed plan. The hearings revealed little opposition to the idea. The institute had bipartisan support in the House Education and Labor Committee, and while it raised the ire of Representative Edith Green, who sought to kill it on the floor of the

House, it reached the conference committee unscathed. The Senate approved a version of the institute, also, and the thirteen differences between the House and Senate provisions proved easy to reconcile in the midst of an otherwise long and stormy conference. Thus the National Institute emerged in 1972 with most of the features the administration had originally proposed.[1 2]

The Emergency School Aid Act that also became part of the 1972 legislation was not precisely the scheme Nixon had recommended, but it had many similarities. Its passage was slowed by the bitter wrangles over busing that nearly paralyzed education law making in the early seventies, and Congress' version attached a few more strings to local school districts than the administration had envisioned, but the president's basic idea—federal funds to cajole and console communities faced with desegregation—survived.[1 3]

The college student aid programs passed in 1972 were as complex and riddled with compromise as any recent domestic legislation. The administration's proposals were nearly lost sight of as senators and representatives tried to resolve their own sizable differences, and in the process some provisions got preserved that the White House wanted to scrap and several others were invented that the administration opposed. Yet the notion of a federally financed resource floor under low-income students did become law—in the amount of $1,400, which was nearly identical to the administration proposal—chiefly because Senate Education Subcommittee chairman Claiborne Pell wanted it and because several powerful members of the House committee did, too. The version that was finally enacted, establishing a new program of Basic Educational Opportunity Grants (BEOG), differed from the Nixon plan in one important technicality: The White House would have had the student scholarships parcelled out by the colleges, albeit under tight government regulations, while the Senate bill provided that the grants would be federally administered as a sort of voucher that the student could use at the college of his choice.[c]

Also retained in the 1972 Amendments, again in modified form, was the notion of a secondary market for student loan paper This would be the new Student Loan Marketing Association.

The National Foundation for Higher Education lost its name and most of its structural features, as well as its initial commitment to foster "excellence," but Congress authorized the secretary of HEW to award a small amount of money to postsecondary institutions for innovation and reform. This became the Fund for the Improvement of Postsecondary Education, lodged in the Office of the Assistant Secretary for Education. Although markedly different from Moynihan's original 1970 conception, it resembled the 1971 version designed by Richardson.

[c]The amount of an individual student's stipend, however, varied with the cost of the particular college he attended, as well as with his own poverty. Three other key student aid programs remained firmly rooted in the campuses.

Continuity and Change

It is tempting for one who participated in the White House working groups of 1969-70 to extract these examples from the Education Amendments of 1972 and use them to argue that Congress recognized the wisdom of the Nixon proposals and, after tinkering with the details, ultimately embraced the basic ideas.

That would be, at the least, an oversimplification. Technically, both the House and Senate committees rejected the administration bills, and the epic legislation that the president finally signed was the product of a series of accommodations between bills that had been written and rewritten on Capitol Hill. It was unmistakeably an act of Congress, not a rubber-stamping of legislation drafted "downtown."

As for those half dozen provisions that resembled the measures the White House had asked for, some will assert this was largely coincidence. None of them was inherently a bad idea, and all were logical steps for the federal government to take in the early seventies. They might have happened even if the Nixon administration had been silent on education.

The White House may unwittingly have improved the prospects for its education program by abandoning interest in it. John Brademas could readily take a proprietary view of the National Institute of Education idea, and Claiborne Pell could credibly identify himself as author of the major new student aid scheme, in part because the presidency was silent. Richard Nixon was not stumping the countryside to promote his education proposals. White House aides were not briefing editors, rallying interest groups, or scouring the corridors of Congress on behalf of them. Toward the end of his tour in Washington, Counselor Moynihan did give a speech to the American Council on Education in which he rebuked the education community for its lack of appreciation of the administration ideas, but by early 1971 he was gone and no one else in the presidential entourage picked up his baton.[14] Between the second round of congressional messages in early 1971 and the final shaping of the legislation a year later, the White House was quiet on the subject of education, save for busing and spending issues. So total, in fact, was this disinterest and so fragmented had White House staff responsibility for education policy become, that officials elsewhere in the executive branch claimed they did not know whom to ask for guidance. One former HEW aide jokes that he sometimes had to call the White House switchboard and ask to be connected to whomever was handling a particular issue that day.[15]

This presidential neglect of education policy allowed others in the administration to fill the vacuum, and some of them had greater credibility on Capitol Hill and within the education community. Elliot Richardson seized and kept the lead, as Robert Finch had never done, and he was ably assisted by others in

HEW, including Commissioner Marland and USOE veteran Peter Muirhead. Their diplomacy was directed both to the congressional committees and staffers at work on the legislation and to the education community's Washington representatives, with whom they held regular meetings.[d]

Others also stepped forward—people in no way linked to the administration—to attest to the desirability of some of the president's proposals. Alice M. Rivlin, then at the Brookings Institution, advised Edith Green's subcommittee that the administration's student aid bill would establish two important principles—the guarantee of assistance to all needy students, and top priority for those least able to pay for college themselves—that the chairman's own rival bill neglected.[16] Rivlin did not say that these were principles she had urged upon the Johnson administration in its waning days or that, largely unbeknown to the Nixon White House, the student aid scheme that Lew Butler had pressed upon the working group in early 1970 derived from the proposals he had inherited from his own HEW predecessor, Alice M. Rivlin. But the lineage did not matter, nor did the administration bill much matter, for the effect of such advice on key members of the House of Representatives was to dispose them, when the time came for conference, to embrace the Senate provisions that were more akin, in spirit and concept, to those Rivlin (and the administration) espoused than were those of Edith Green.

In John Brademas' hearings on the National Institute of Education, it was not only Moynihan and the administration that testified in favor of the proposal. Two respected former education commissioners from the Kennedy-Johnson era, Francis Keppel and Harold Howe II, also came to Washington to endorse the institute idea in glowing terms.

When the time came for comment on the proposed "secondary market," again the administration was not a voice in the wilderness. The American Bankers Association was quick "to endorse and, indeed, urge the establishment of a viable facility such as the National Student Loan Association."[17] Even the luckless National Foundation for Higher Education picked up a little support from educators who took another look at the idea, particularly as revised in 1971, and found some features of it that they liked.

Whereas the White House is apt to work overtime to elicit such endorsements of measures that hold a high priority for the president, there is no evidence that anyone in the administration orchestrated the testimony in 1971. Many of those giving it would have rebuffed any such attempt, for the reason they bothered to testify at all was not that they wanted to boost the chances of

[d]Within moments of Moynihan's October 1970 address, ACE Chairman Arthur S. Flemming rose to accept his challenge to meet with the administration. "If the federal government will designate the time and place," Flemming promised, "we will provide the leaders on our side and shall be prepared to do so as early as next week." In little more than a week, the first such meeting was held, and Richardson diligently kept them going. See Arthur S. Flemming, "Response to Mr. Moynihan," in W. Todd Furniss, ed., *Higher Education for Everybody?* Washington, D.C., American Council on Education, 1971, pp. 255-57.

favorable treatment for a Nixon initiative—to the contrary—but that they saw merit in some of the proposals or at least in the principles undergirding them.

This may be the working definition of an "idea whose time has come" in Washington, one that transcends its immediate origins and wins the support of many who find it to their own liking, or in their own interest, even if they care not at all about the fate of the idea's own sponsors. The point here is simply that some of the administration's ideas appeared to be of that genre, and that White House apathy toward its own proposals may, in the political climate of Washington in the early seventies, have made it easier for others to claim them as their own or to endorse them without regard to their source.

Presidential diffidence certainly contributed to the nonpartisan climate in which education policy was made in 1970-1972. The concurrent issues of busing, appropriations, and campus unrest allowed for plenty of political posturing, but the substantive program changes were considered in a fairly quiet atmosphere and seldom decided by party-line votes. Had the administration kept them spotlighted as Republican initiatives, approval might have been more elusive.

Gauging the originality of a policy idea may be a futile exercise. By the time one reaches the president's pen for signature, it is apt to have multiple sources that a day in the library would reveal, although the elected official, unfamiliar with the professional literature and trusting the advice of eager aides, may genuinely believe that no one ever thought of it before. One or more commissions, task forces, and advisory groups will have suggested it. Previous administrations will have aired it. National associations will have sought it. Candidates will have promised it. Journalists will have weighed it. On any given day in any given policy realm there are plenty of ideas waiting to be seized. The interesting question, then, is not where the president (or the Congress) found the ideas, or whether they invented them *de novo*, but which ones were seized and why. Were they modest alterations or sweeping overhauls? Costly or inexpensive? Progressive or reactionary? Would they move the government into uncharted terrain, add fresh detail to familiar maps or correct the errors of earlier cartographers?

The Amendments of 1972, like the Nixon proposals of 1970, had some provisions with all of these features, but their general thrust was to move the nation closer to goals that it had earlier set for itself but not yet attained. The White House would never admit it, but it had provided fresh ammunition to those who believe that national social policy is nearly always incremental.

The New Federalism and The Great Society

In education, as in most other domestic spheres, the basic question awaiting the new Republican administration was what to do with the policy legacy of eight years of Democratic hegemony. The national government had been involved with education since the late eighteenth century, but the principal programs it sponsored in 1969 had either begun or been substantially revised during the decade just ending. Lincoln had signed the Morrill Act in 1862, to be sure, Truman the G.I. Bill, and Eisenhower the National Defense Education Act, but the shape of the federal education effort had mostly been determined while Kennedy and Johnson inhabited the White House, especially during the years when Lyndon B. Johnson, the self-styled education president, occupied the Oval Office.

Many felt the programs had not lived up to their promise. Poor people still found college too expensive. Disadvantaged youngsters still lagged behind their grade level. High school and college graduates still found themselves lacking in employable skills. Educational researchers had not yet figured out how children really learn, let alone how public policy could usefully intervene in the process to help them learn more. Schools and colleges were still too often dull and rigid places. People from middle- and upper-class families continued to fare better in school and afterwards than their lower-class agemates. Black and white youngsters mostly still sat in classrooms where everyone was the same color.

The new administration had to decide whether to abandon the goals and scrap the programs, keep the goals and alter the programs, or head in new directions and devise new programs in order to get there. With rare exceptions, the Nixon White House began by selecting the middle course, retaining—though sometimes also rephrasing—the objectives and seeking moderate changes in the specific programs intended to reach them. There was no abrupt broadening or narrowing of the definition of the federal role in education. Where a program was marked for extinction, it was generally either one that previous administrations had also found fault with, such as aid to "federally impacted areas," or one that was to be immersed in a larger effort, such as the categorical schemes Nixon proposed to fold into the National Foundation for Higher Education.

With time the policy alterations would become more drastic, notably in the 1971 proposal for education revenue sharing. And in the realm of school desegregation, it must be said that the administration's new programs of encouragement followed fruitless efforts to stalemate the whole process in the courts. In the main, however, the transition from Johnson to Nixon brought no sharp discontinuity in the education goals pursued by the executive branch of the federal government. No attempt was made to abolish the large compensatory programs such as Title I and Head Start at the elementary and secondary level, nor was there any retreat from the goal of boosting opportunity for the poor to attend college. The constant battle between the White House and Congress over how much to spend on education programs tended to eclipse the policy continuity of the programs themselves. Also, Nixon's rhetoric of "reform," particularly in elementary and secondary education, and his insistence on judging the schools by their results heralded more of a change in policy than the administration's substantive proposals actually delivered. Those scrutinizing the actual legislative language instead of the rhetoric of the president's messages would have discovered that the Republican administration had not set out to repeal the Great Society's education policies so much as to make them work better.

Why the continuity? Three partial explanations may be suggested.

First, unlike those policy realms where the national government is dominant, in education the federal role had always been sharply limited, even during an activist Democratic regime. The Republican White House could shade and reinterpret that role, but if it tried drastically to change the script or assume direction of the whole show, it would find itself unceremoniously ushered off stage. Highly decentralized and resistant to change, the educational system simply did not present a very promising aspect to a new administration eager to put its own stamp on the life of the nation.

Second, the people who reviewed education policy for Richard Nixon were generally comfortable with established federal objectives, if uneasy with details of program and structure. They were not disposed to steer the administration away from a commitment to equal opportunity, which in one form or another undergirded most of the government's extant education activities. Some, such as Moynihan, had helped to shape the Great Society. Others, such as the career officials in HEW and the Budget Bureau who assisted Butler, Allen, and Nathan, displayed both the institutional commitment to stability and gradual change that characterizes the permanent government and, in many cases, also a personal commitment to the goals of programs they knew so well. Some had taken part in Johnson administration policy reviews, such as that carried out under Alice Rivlin's direction, that would likely have shaped administration policy if the Democrats had retained the presidency in 1968. They were able, by virtue of their own continuity, to intrude the same ideas into the early thinking of the Republican regime.

Third, the combination of a president who initially fancied himself a reformer of Johnsonian programs rather than an eraser of their objectives, a Democratic Congress that was unlikely to respond favorably to sharp detours in federal education policy, the paucity of arresting new program ideas in circles frequented by administration officials, the tendency of the White House to make its policy behind closed doors, and the ceaseless distraction of other issues, all militated against nonincremental change.

Once its course was set, administration policy changed very little. Apart from the unrequited flirtation with education revenue sharing, the ideas the president voiced in 1970, as modified in 1971, animated the executive branch approach to education for the next six years, surviving even the fall of Richard Nixon and the rise of Gerald Ford in 1974. The passage of major legislation in 1972 and again in 1974 had little effect on the administration, which doggedly pursued its own conception of which programs were worth supporting and employed the budget, appropriation vetoes, refusals to spend money, and outright footdragging in stubborn attempts to carry out its ideas.

This pattern ultimately took on a ritualistic character that sometimes became quite silly. Each year the White House would decline to request any money for the programs it disliked while seeking large sums for those it favored. Each year the interest groups would voice their outrage and then turn their attention to Capitol Hill where each year the Congress would rewrite the education budget.

Aid for college students was the main rope in this tug-of-war. The administration ascertained that the program of Basic Educational Opportunity Grants came closest to carrying out its top priority, which was to help the lowest-income students gain access to higher education, so every January the president's budget would include a healthy amount for that program, nothing at all for two of the popular "campus-based" aid programs, and reduced funds for the third one. Every year Congress acted as though no student aid budget had even been submitted, and proceeded to fashion its own. In time, a former official who had had to defend the president's requests would term the administration's policy "doubtful on substantive grounds" and "a disaster politically."[18] But as the 1976 election campaign got under way, it was still the administration's policy.

The chief reason for this remarkable durability is simply that, for all practical purposes, the administration had stopped thinking about education. The working groups that Morgan had chaired in 1969-70 were the first and last of their kind in the field of education, and for the next six years the White House virtually disregarded the subject, save when a specific problem arose. Policy stopped being made; it was simply executed. Issues were generally resolved within the appropriate agency or with the help of the Office of Management and Budget (formerly the Bureau of the Budget). Ideas that portended changes in policy were rejected out of hand, just as programs that seemed to clash with the administration's priorities went unbudgeted or their funds uncommitted for as long as possible.

Nixon and Johnson: Process and Politics

The Nixon education messages appeared less than five years after Lyndon Johnson had signed the landmark Elementary and Secondary and Higher Education Acts. The Great Society legislation, with its scope, its ambitious levels of authorized spending, the breadth of its appeal, the popularity of its programs, and the adroitness with which they had been assembled inevitably set the standard by which the next president's education policies would be judged.

In any such competition, the men who devised the earlier proposals started with a trio of advantages: (1) a relatively empty slate on which any scribblings would be readily visible and from which little needed to be erased in order to make room for new entries; (2) the knowledge that some "new money" was to be had, for the domestic side of the budget was ballooning and—until the costs of the Vietnam War changed all—the president assigned a high priority to education spending; and (3) the fact that their party controlled both houses of the Congress that would have to pass upon any legislative initiatives. Any program they designed thus had the benefit of novelty to make it dramatic, resources to make it alluring, and votes to make it susceptible of passage. Of course they also had a president who was interested in their results.

The Nixon working groups, by contrast, started with a legacy of ongoing programs, with the assumption that little additional money was going to be budgetted for their proposals, at least in the near term, and with the glum certainty that continued Democratic control of Congress would make any Republican initiative difficult to enact. The protracted tussle with Congress over the size of the 1970 appropriation, soon overtaken by a similar battle over the 1971 figures, aggravated all these conditions and cast a shadow over the entire process of executive branch education policy development. The president's own spotty interest in the subject did nothing to improve morale or to encourage the invention of bold new programs.

Chroniclers of the Johnson education bills, particularly the ESEA, have made much of the administration's use of outside experts in conceiving the original proposals; of the fruitful interaction of officials from USOE, the upper echelons of HEW, the White House, and the Budget Bureau in assembling ideas, brokering them with interest groups, and resolving political and substantive dilemmas; of the imagination shown in putting together a package of seemingly unrelated programs in a way that sidestepped old obstacles, meshed the conflicting aspirations of powerful lobbies, and gained momentum from association with the War on Poverty; and of the political savvy that enabled them quickly to push through Congress the delicately balanced structure of compromises for which they had obtained prior clearance from the major constituencies.[19] In a remarkable demonstration of legislative and political ingenuity, helped on by adroit timing, the Johnson team burst through the three historic barriers of "Red, Religion, and Race" that had blocked so many previous proposals.

Yet while the Johnson education program may have needed political skill for enactment, its goals were immensely popular. Although Congress was more sluggish, public opinion had long since accepted the idea of federal aid to education. Johnson's genius lay in assembling a package which attained that end without antagonizing the powerful forces that had defeated earlier attempts.

In elementary and secondary education, by contrast, the Nixon program rhetorically assaulted the school establishment itself and did so in the name of a theory—more precisely a body of data—that probably fewer than a thousand people in the nation understood at the time. Whatever the common-sense appeal of the Moynihan-Coleman analysis to people who sensed they were spending more on schools and not necessarily getting any more education in return, the call for better research was not one destined for popular acclaim.

In higher education, the administration's core proposal—a careful targetting of federal funds on low-income students—was based on a straightforward notion of progressive social policy, rather than a theory about pedagogy, but it was not designed to appeal to the traditional Republican constituency, to college officials anxious about their institutional account books, or to a nation beginning to evince greater interest in the difficulties facing the middle-class family trying to pay for higher education. The National Foundation idea rested on a cogent enough philosophy about the proper relationship between Washington and the nation's universities, but it promised little fiscal relief to the campuses and, by proposing to end some familiar programs, alarmed those educators who mistrusted the administration's intentions or were unprepared to take their chances with an unknown agency.

Yet the analyses behind these proposals were intended to make a kind of abstract good sense to the public, whether the professionals liked them or not. Where Johnson's aides had spent endless hours negotiating with the lobbyists, the Nixon administration sought to reach over the obvious interest groups to convey a message to "Everyman" about the nation's educational system, about what he should expect of it, and about the proper role of the national government in relation to it. Characteristically, the process of formulating that message largely bypassed the professionals within the executive branch most familiar with the desires and sensitivities of the interest groups and omitted any serious attention to the views of congressmen who were apt to think themselves the most accurate mirrors of the electorate's wishes.

The three classic constituencies for a federal program—the "not so holy Trinities" as they were once called—are the interest groups directly affected by it, the executive branch officials who administer it, and the congressmen and committee staff aides who specialize in that policy realm and dominate the process by which an idea gets enacted.

The Johnson White House had made extensive use of all three groups in formulating its education programs. Outside advisory panels generated ideas; legislative specifications emerged from the Office of Education; key members of Congress were courted and their views solicited. The White House supervised this process, imposing its own ideas when needed, but mindful of the penultimate pragmatic test: Could an idea be turned into law? (The final test—Would the program work?—was less often invoked.)

The Nixon working groups behaved rather differently. Preoccupied with internal consensus, constrained by the president's penchant for surprise, and doubtful that the political climate would permit their proposals, no matter how sensible, to elicit a warm reception from Congress or the professional educators, they rarely sought the participation of career officials, interest group spokesmen, or denizens of Capitol Hill, even those of their own party.

Educators and Interest Groups

President Nixon's own preinaugural task force on education, chaired by Carnegie Corporation President Alan Pifer, had delicately observed that no entries in his previous record "have served to identify him personally with education" and, "speaking candidly," noted that "we do not believe that President-elect Nixon, with all his varied and high qualifications for office, would at present by most Americans be considered to have the kind of special concern for education the times require."[20] Simply stated, American educators had no reason to expect much from the Nixon administration; to the contrary, his old reputation as a red-baiter in Congress, his record as the Vice President who broke a Senate tie on a school-aid bill in 1959 by voting against it, and his distance from the liberal establishment that molds the conventional wisdom on national education issues all signalled trouble.

Yet the new administration did not bolt the door to educators and their views and in several instances might even be said to have courted them for a time. First, there was the preinaugural task force itself, consisting not only of Pifer but also such other luminaries as Stephen Bailey, Lawrence Cremin, Clark Kerr, Francis Keppel, Allen Wallis, and Meredith Wilson. It was very much an establishment group.

Before its first year was out, the administration had summoned another advisory group of educators, the President's Task Force on Higher Education, which Arthur Burns organized and which consisted of sixteen well-known college presidents and others. And the administration's own upper echelons contained such academic and educational figures as Burns, Moynihan, DuBridge, Kissinger, Shultz, and Allen.

It could not be said that the professional advice of educators was never sought. Indeed, in several important particulars the messages Nixon dispatched to Capitol Hill in March 1970 bore their stamp, although those most heeded were not institutional spokesmen or organized interest groups so much as individual analysts drawn from within the academy. The underlying rationale for the entire elementary and secondary education message came straight from the Coleman Report and the protracted reanalysis that Moynihan and other social scientists had put it through in the late sixties. Coleman himself read and made suggestions for early drafts of the president's message. The National Foundation for Higher Education, in concept if not in detail, was borrowed from the Carnegie Commission on Higher Education and Moynihan did not shy from acknowledging that lineage. Other ideas were tested out on informal groups of education experts, including those at the Harvard Graduate School of Education whom I consulted while working on the presidential messages.

But the White House did not publicize these contacts and, more important-ly, it did not court the Washington representatives of the many education associations that viewed themselves as national spokesmen for the interests of the schools, the colleges, and—they intimated—the nation's youth.

Some dissembling may be found on both sides of this point, with the lobbyists charging that they were never invited to participate and with administration officials retorting that they never offered, but that debate is secondary. Three other considerations are central: First, administration officials had no intention of framing their education policy proposals around the desires of educators, any more than they constructed their welfare reform plan around the wishes of social workers. Domestic policy during that period of Nixon's tenure had a near-populist and antiprofessional thrust. Second, issues of visceral importance to many outside the White House gates often elicited a more cerebral approach from the president's advisors. The working groups debated principles, philosophies, and ideas about matters that most educators saw in terms of money, personnel, institutional stability, even survival. Third, the political relations between the White House and the education fraternity had been unhappy since the first appropriations contretemps of mid-1969. Two consecutive presidential vetoes of education money bills formed the backdrop for these relations, and long before the administration unveiled its substantive policy proposals it was perceived as hostile to the interests of teachers and professors.

This situation reinforced the tendency of many high-level administration officials to regard educators as hostile to the Nixon presidency, as simply another self-interested group eager to batten on the taxpayer's dollar with scant regard for the efficacy of those funds in achieving the stated objectives of the programs through which they flowed. Certainly the evidence was mounting that the sorts of policy measures many well-meaning educators had said would enhance student achievement and equal opportunity had less effect than had been hoped. Such findings had found no eager audience in the education profession, and the profession's disregard of them found few admirers in the Nixon working groups. A year before joining the White House staff, Moynihan had written with some acerbity that the education establishment's response to the Coleman findings was a "policy of silence."[21]

In addition, forces external to the making of education policy cannot be wholly discounted. The Vietnam War was still in full swing, and students and their teachers were prominent among those rallying outside the White House gates to denounce the president who persisted with that folly. College deans explained to the world that the reason their campuses were awash with protest and disruption was the malevolent foreign policy of that man in the White House and its domestic correlates such as the military draft. Nixon was to respond in kind, reportedly ordering in 1971 that MIT's federal contracts be cut back in order to punish Jerome Wiesner's opposition to his policies. The Cambodian incursion followed the education messages by a matter of weeks, and from then on the relations between presidential loyalists and the preponderance of the nation's educators could most charitably be described as icy. But even while the working groups were molding the content of those messages, few in the White House believed there was much political mileage to be gotten from casting the administration's education policy so as to appeal to the interest groups professionally responsible for education.

Two related observations may be ventured: in the realm of elementary and secondary education, for all the modest incrementalism of the administration's substantive proposals, the thrust of the working group's Coleman-based analysis was that a substantial portion of professional education dogma was wrong and that it was the president's proper role to say so. "President Nixon had declared what amounts to a limited war on the educational establishment" was the way one Washington journalist characterized the bellicose tone of the Message to Congress.[22] Given that most educators would not change their views simply because Richard Nixon told them to, it was thought necessary to reach beyond them to the people whose children were in school and whose taxes paid for schools and to convey a message to them that the education fraternity either did not agree with or did not find serviceable to embrace.

When they turned to higher education, however, members of the working group were less disposed to find fault or to demand reform. Perhaps because several of them were college professors, they softened the critical tone of their comments on the public schools and instead paid some attention to the likely audience reaction. While the decision not to urge a new federal program of institutional aid would find few friends among college administrators, the forceful advocacy of equal opportunity and the emphasis upon assistance for impoverished students might reasonably be expected to gain support. Similarly the new National Foundation, combined with the stress on federal nonintervention in campus affairs, was consonant with what working group members thought many educators would—or, more precisely, should—want. Had not the idea of the foundation been lifted from the Carnegie Commission? Ironically, at least in part because of the assumption that these proposals would be popular, working group members may have felt relieved of any burden to make advance overtures designed to curry favor.

Commissioner Allen knew better, and his unease with both messages flowed at least in part from his perception of what his professional colleagues wanted and his understanding of the tactics best suited to sway them. Allen did not disagree with the substance of the administration's concrete proposals, but he sensed more clearly than his fellow working group members that the pugnacious rhetoric, the mode of presentation, the lack of consultation, and the absence of large new financial commitments would dwarf the merits of the specific recommendations in the eyes of the education fraternity. More than his working group colleagues—indeed, *alone* among them—he found that prospect troubling.

Finally, it may be noted that the administration failed to make explicit use of the reports of either of the two prestigious educational task forces that it had established or to mobilize their members as missionaries for its proposals. While most of the president's proposals, so far as they went, were congruent with recommendations of Alan Pifer's transition task force and James Hester's panel on higher education (although both groups also made numerous recommendations that were not echoed in the White House messages), it never occurred to anyone in the working group or, so far as can be discerned, anyone else in the administration to emphasize that kinship. Indeed, the Pifer report was never even released by the White House (although it appeared in the *Congressional Record* in early 1969) and the Hester Report was embargoed until six months after the president's messages were dispatched to Capitol Hill. Whereas President Johnson recalled in his memoirs that "a coalition of support" for his program "was carefully built up among educational institutions and other interested groups," Richard Nixon could make no such claim in his autobiography.[23]

The Office of Education

Describing the genesis of the Elementary and Secondary Education Act, Stephen K. Bailey highlighted the "seminal and pervasive influence" of Education Commissioner Francis Keppel.[24] The former dean of the Harvard School of Education, Keppel was an adroit negotiator, enjoyed ready access to the White House, was perceived by his constituency as a major figure in determining administration education policy, and had several years of experience in his position before the legislation was unveiled. Although Johnson's bills were shaped by many hands, it is fair to say that much of their substance emerged from the agencies that would administer the programs.

Almost the opposite situation prevailed in the Nixon administration. Insofar as USOE officials shared at all in the development of education policies, their role was chiefly that of reacting to the views and ideas of others in the administration. Insofar as the White House listened to HEW, it was Butler, Patricelli, and others in the Office of the Secretary whose views were usually heeded.

Why this should be so has to be considered on several levels. Some senior members of the Nixon administration were undeniably suspicious of the career civil service that, it was felt, filled the bureaucracy with Democrats hostile to Richard Nixon. Nathan has dubbed this attitude the "anti-bureaucracy administration."[25] In the case of agencies devoted to human resource programs, such as HEW, this suspicion mounted, for many of the men near the president believed that these departments were ruled by the liberal convictions characteristic of persons who favor such activities. Even among the administration's own appointees, those in HEW, OEO, the Labor Department and a few other domestic agencies were believed to harbor views to the left of the president's.

Such suspicions were not entirely without foundation. Secretary Finch was patently "the liberal" in the original Nixon cabinet, many of his associates hailed from the progressive wing of the Republican Party, the civil service did contain thousands whose convictions were shaped by the policies and programs of eight years of Democratic leadership, and the HEW rolls naturally included many who were sympathetic to the goals of the programs they ran and the clienteles they served.

At the White House, the deepest mistrust was reserved for agency employees who, in addition to being careerists running Democratic-inspired social welfare programs in "liberal" departments, could also be said to represent a particular outside interest group, especially one that did not support the Nixon administration.

Several agencies qualified for that distinction, but none more so than the U.S. Office of Education, which during the century of its existence had naturally become the unit within the executive branch that the nation's educators expected to look out for their interests.

That most educators had little use for Nixon seemed clear. Nearly 60 percent of the nation's college professors had voted for Humphrey in 1968—compared with 43 percent of the national electorate[26]—and within months of the Republican victory the principal school lobbies had banded together to breach the president's budget.[e] There was no reason to suppose that the career educators employed by USOE felt differently, and Commissioner Allen's feckless attempts to bring in new faces at the political level did not include many Republicans.

There is a sad irony here, for one major source of Allen's failure to play a larger role in administration policy making was the thinness of his own top staff; yet the principal reason he had so few capable and trusted senior associates was that one candidate after another had been rejected by the political clearance process in HEW and the White House. Whether there is an acute shortage of able Republican educators in the land or whether Allen simply never found them is open to dispute, but there can be little question that his frustrated attempts to recruit staff left him short-handed at the same time as they reinforced the administration's suspicion that all educators, and those who worked on education within the government, were politically questionable.[f]

The Office of Education's relations within HEW were also uneasy. The planners, analysts, and liaison men in the Office of the Secretary—a misleading term for what was itself a sizable bureaucracy within a larger one—were contemptuous of the program managers across the street. Yet men such as Butler, Patricelli, and Under Secretary John Veneman had excellent working relationships that had been forged during the development of the welfare reform

---

[e]As noted earlier, the fiscal 1970 budget had been written in Johnson's Budget Bureau, but as of January 20, 1969, it belonged to Nixon, and he chose not to augment the portions of it that dealt with education.

[f]A long and happy exception was the cordial working relationship between Allen's executive assistant, Gregory Anrig, and myself. We talked several times a day, liked and respected one another, and did our best to keep open a mutually beneficial "working-level link" between the White House and the Office of Education even at times when our principals had little contact.

plan in mid-1969 with Morgan, Moynihan, Nathan, and other Executive Office aides who worked on education.

White House staffers understandably preferred to deal with HEW as a single entity, expected those in the secretary's entourage to resolve whatever differences might arise within the department, and when faced with the need to call someone at HEW about a matter were disposed to dial a person thought to speak for the whole agency rather than one of its subsidiary parts. That most of those receiving such calls were lawyers—generalists—rather than specialists in a particular subject also bespeaks the administration's tendency to assume that "experts" could not have a sufficiently dispassionate or "presidential" perspective.

Even under different conditions, it would have been remarkable if the Office of Education had taken the lead in developing policies that, while built on goals the government had long accepted, were also critical of previous federal attempts to deal with the nation's educational condition and none too sympathetic to the stated desires of educational leaders. Worse, the ongoing strife over appropriations for current programs and the modest budget assumptions built into the new proposals dampened the enthusiasm of officials whose own status and morale largely reflect the priority the White House assigns their domain when dollars are being distributed. Worse still, two of the president's leading proposals—the National Institute of Education and the Foundation for Higher Education—would transfer large areas of responsibility to new agencies set up outside of the Office of Education. Bureaucracies seldom respond enthusiastically to threats of this sort.

But if the commissioner of education and his top aides did not originate the contents of the presidential messages and did not exhaust themselves in promoting the ideas, neither did they publicly dissent. Much as Allen wanted the Budget Bureau to locate additional money for the nation's hard-pressed schools and colleges, he too was a reformer who welcomed the idea of a National Institute of Education, endorsed the principle of targetting federal student aid on the neediest, and favored the emphasis on change in the two presidential messages. At least he did after some of the harsh first draft rhetoric was muted. Although he was visibly unhappy with the administration's overall spending priorities and deeply pained by the president's waffling and foot dragging on school desegregation, Allen saw much merit in the analyses set forth in the two messages. When the AFT's Selden urged him to resign in protest, the commissioner replied that "the proposals contained in the President's Message on Educational Reform are highly constructive and long overdue." While they did not "substitute [sic] nor diminish the need for increased financial support," Allen wrote, they were nonetheless "essential for the long-term strength of education in our country and they deserve the full support of every member of the profession."

The Congress

There is little to be said about administration efforts to involve members of Congress in the design of education policies, for practically no effort was made. Legislative liaison men did not participate in either of the working groups; hence any information about what key members of Congress or their aides might recommend and about the likely reception of ideas being considered at the White House was secondhand at best.

Officials at HEW strove to maintain channels of communication with Capitol Hill, but this was not made any easier by the working groups' penchant for surprise or by the recurrent quarrels over spending levels. In the early autumn of 1969, it may be recalled, the entire education message had been intended to divert congressional attention from the appropriations veto and to equip Finch and Allen with something constructive to say when they went up to explain the administration's stance.

Working group members were not unaware of Congress, but simply paid it scant heed. The fact that both Senate and House had sizable Democratic majorities and that every committee and subcommittee was therefore chaired by a Democrat was fundamental. Why waste time consulting with the opposition? And why, for that matter, devote much energy to Republicans whose limited ardor for administration ideas would still not muster enough votes to enact them? If the president's ideas had integrity and made sense to the nation, Congress would come around. If it did not, at least the president would have made sense. His own wisdom could be trumpetted, and he could always add education to his growing list of initiatives ready to be hauled out when it seemed advantageous to belabor Congress for its hostility to sensible reform.

If Morgan and his colleagues had thought more about it, they might have realized that this cavalier handling of the legislative branch would win no friends for the president. What they could not have so readily foreseen was that it would contribute to the heightened suspicions that led Congress to write education laws in the early 1970s in unprecedented detail, full of obsessive safeguards meant to constrain the executive's freedom of action. In thus contributing to the demise of the "Imperial Presidency" and the renaissance of Congress, the education working groups left a further legacy of extraordinarily ponderous programs and needlessly intricate regulations that would themselves emerge as a serious problem a scant few years later.

In the event, neither prophesy nor congressional relations was the responsibility of Morgan and his colleagues. Their task was to advise the president on the content of his education policy.

Groupthink in Domestic Policy

In carrying out the task of advising the president, the education working groups
had a singular context and behavior pattern of their own, not unlike that found
by Irving L. Janis in his classic study of policy task forces in the foreign affairs
field. Indeed, one could detect analogs to most of the major symptoms that
Janis associates with the "groupthink syndrome," though these were displayed
sporadically rather than constantly, with varying degrees of severity and with
some notable exceptions:[27]

1. "An illusion of invulnerability" was certainly shared by many working
group members, manifesting itself in the presumption that no one was better
able than they to diagnose the nation's educational ills, in the belief that getting
the president to voice certain policies was a worthwhile end in itself and in the
expectation that the nation would heed his words and adjust its views
accordingly.

2. "Collective efforts to rationalize" the wisdom and veracity of the group's
own assumptions could also be detected, along with a tendency "to discount
warnings" that those assumptions might lead to flawed or infeasible policies.
Sometimes the rationalizations took the form of a too-easy acceptance of
constraints: "Within the available budget resources, this is the best that anyone
could do." "Talking to others about this idea would violate the president's desire
for bold surprises." In other instances, the working groups took refuge in
appealing catch words such as "reform," "excellence," and "equal opportunity,"
in simple extrapolation of concepts that made sense in other contexts (e.g.,
"income" rather than "services," "outcomes" rather than "expenditures") and
in the unexamined belief that because a single expert or national panel had
embraced an idea, others would laud the president for proposing it.

3. "An unquestioned belief in the group's inherent morality." Since everyone in the room knew he wanted only good things for the nation's schoolchildren, it was inconceivable that whatever decisions the group reached could
portend anything but desirable results.

4. "Stereotyped views of enemy leaders as too evil to warrant genuine
attempts to negotiate . . . ." While depicting education spokesmen, the Congress,
or the bureaucracy as "enemies" exaggerates the working group's animus toward
them, certainly the leaders of the "unholy trinity" were not thought susceptible
to genuine negotiation.

5. "Direct pressure on any member who expresses strong arguments against
any of the group's stereotypes, illusions, or commitments . . . ." In their early
phases, the working groups enjoyed a lively give and take of ideas. But
individuals who dissented too loudly from the evolving consensus encountered
mounting pressure, ranging from Morgan's decision to exclude Roger Freeman,
to Moynihan's pointed rebuttal of Lew Butler's doubts about the National
Foundation, to the quiet signals passed to Commissioner Allen that if he wanted

his favorite ideas and principles embodied in the presidential messages he should stop agitating for more money.

6. "Self-censorship of deviation from the apparent group consensus." As his spirited last-minute memorandum of appeal to the president demonstrates, Allen did not submit to rigorous self-censorship of his own views, and Morgan's willingness to report split votes in the higher education decision memorandum indicates that the working group format did not demand total consensus. Yet most members seemed to have taken a tacit vow of obedience to the group norms, confining their dissents to the conference room, declining to use outside channels to win allies who might help sway the president's decisions in their favor, and willingly partaking of shared self-delusions such as the National Foundation's ability to effect a dozen disparate goals.

The two final symptoms in Janis' account—"a shared illusion of unanimity" and "the emergence of self-appointed mindguards"—were not much in evidence around Morgan's conference table. A more telling feature of "groupthink," and one that went beyond the panels assigned to education policy, was a generalized willingness to keep the office door closed. Whereas sensitive foreign policy deliberations may demand secrecy, domestic policy development does not. Yet tight lips and shut doors characterized this phase of the administration's approach to domestic affairs. In earlier months, the Urban Affairs Council mechanism had shoved the windows open from time to time, if only because its frequent meetings of cabinet-level officials were known to the press and thus compelled occasional briefings on what transpired in those sessions. But when the transition to Ehrlichman (and later the Domestic Council) brought an end to such gatherings, the celebrated "passion for anonymity" of White House staffers, the president's fondness for unveiling surprises, and the peculiar dynamics of the "decision memorandum" process made for a minimum of outside participation and scrutiny. When one is preparing a set of options for a reclusive president, when one has few indications of which he will choose, and when aiming toward a Message to Congress that will highlight his preferences, one has obvious incentives not to expose the unresolved choices to others whose discretion and loyalty cannot be assumed and whose self-interests are entangled.

This, too, was easily rationalized with terms such as "reform," which imply that familiar solutions to familiar dilemmas were flawed, that the usual array of experts, interest groups, and bureaucrats were incapable of devising or accepting thoroughgoing changes, and that a carefully designed and forcefully stated set of alternatives would command favor with the nation as a whole. Once one believes that, it is but a short step to the corollary view: Freshness of perspective and integrity of analysis will be vitiated by trying to satisfy too many interests, and prospects for a favorable reception will be harmed by letting those who are themselves part of the problem have advance warning about the solution. In sum, the White House evinced a peculiar blend of populism and authoritarianism, of good intentions and haughty self-righteousness. In time, of course, the reformist and populist thrust would dissipate, and where the early months of the Nixon administration were characterized by a number of imaginative domestic policy proposals, in its later days only the authoritarianism and self-righteousness, still cloaked in secrecy, would remain.

6 Education and the Presidency

Presidents seldom think about education. While educators may find this hard to accept, matters of arresting importance to them get no regular or sustained attention inside the Oval Office. As seen from the White House, education is a low-level issue that commands no precedence on the ever-lengthening list of presidential concerns. It probably ranks with housing and nutrition, which is to say it gets more heed than Indian affairs and mental health, but less than welfare, energy, or pollution. These hierarchies change over time, to be sure, and events may catapult a low-visibility subject to momentary prominence, but with the exception of the Johnson White House in 1964-65, education has never stood high on the list for very long.

Why should this be so? Fifty-nine million Americans are enrolled in schools and colleges, and another three million are employed to teach them. Nearly one-third of the population could be said to have education as its primary activity, and when their relatives are counted it could fairly be said that no other "industry," public or private, has the attention of more people. Yet at 1600 Pennsylvania Avenue, where the great concerns of the nation regularly come to roost, education is most often conspicuous by its absence, notwithstanding that the federal government now invests many billions of dollars a year in the activities of this industry and notwithstanding the large number of ex-professors usually found on the president's staff.

No interest group would welcome the lowly status symbolized by White House inattention, and educators habitually offer a dual explanation for it: first, that a given president and his advisors do not *care* about education, and, second, that the federal government is so poorly organized that no one who does care about it has the rank and access to the Oval Office that would compel even a heedless chief executive to give the subject its due.

Both complaints have some validity, but they do not adequately account for the situation. At least four additional explanations need also be considered.

First, presidents practically always spend most of their time and energy on such ineluctable responsibilities as foreign relations, national defense, the condition of the economy, party leadership, and congressional relations. Stephen Hess estimates that "as much as two-thirds" of the president's time is devoted just to foreign affairs.[1] Not much remains for the substance of domestic social policy.

Second, within the broad spectrum of domestic concerns, presidents naturally concentrate on issues where the federal role is dominant, where

Washington's leverage is substantial, and where they are apt to be held accountable for the outcome. "Political leadership," Richard Rose observes, "is leadership by exception. Only by ignoring *almost* everything the government does can the President find time and resources in which to identify and pursue a finite number of political objectives of his own."[2] Education rarely falls within that number. Reserved to the states by the Tenth Amendment, the nation's schools and colleges look to Washington for just ten cents out of every dollar in their budgets. Practically nobody holds the president responsible for the caliber of history teaching at the local high school or the job placement record of the nearby state college. Significantly, when presidents do attend to education, they are apt to focus on politically sensitive aspects of it, such as school desegregation, where the federal role is prominent. Otherwise, it is a marginal activity of the national government—those billions constitute less than 5 percent of the budget—and one where Washington has marginal impact. Presidents have little time for such matters, given the lively competition for their attention by numerous issues where the federal role is clear and decisive.

Third, most federal activity in the field of education is ancillary to other national interests. Only a handful of the many programs that touch education are explicitly "educational" in their origin and intent. The rest generally get dealt with in their primary contexts—that is, as facets of science policy, veterans policy, defense policy, income maintenance, manpower and the like. Not surprisingly, their impact on education, while often substantial, tends to be seen from the White House as incidental.

This perception bolsters the educators' claim that the structure of the executive branch works against their interests, that education programs are numerous and fragmented, and because no one is "in charge" of the whole subject, the president finds it too easy to ignore. But in fact, the underlying reason for this situation is not structural; it is the derivative character of the federal interest in education itself and the fact that most of the myriad programs began as attempts to assist the nation to achieve quite different goals. No single grand enactment encompasses federal activity in this realm. Unlike Social Security, defense procurement, foreign aid, and many other federal domains, education policy has no legislative focal point, nothing to crystallize attention, no identifiable act of Congress that lends itself to comprehensive amendment or homogeneous administration.

Fourth, presidents see scant political reward for spending time on education, apart from paying regular obeisance to its "apple pie" characteristics. To be sure, no chief executive in his right mind would say unkind things about the "three Rs," would refuse to proclaim National Education Week, or fail to laud the Teacher of the Year. But presidents discern little gain from doing much more than being superficially affirmative. Because the federal role in education is so confined, the subject rarely looms as a consequential issue in national elections, at least in the eyes of ordinary voters, and to date the education profession has not wielded much clout at the polls. Although this seems to be changing as a consequence of the growing militance of the large teachers' associations, thus far their impact has been stronger in congressional races. As the palpable inattention to education by both Carter and Ford in 1976 attests, presidential candidates have not yet had reason to believe that their prospects for election much depend on their actions or statements in this field.

Withal, presidents cannot completely ignore it, for education does become entangled with large national concerns, and federal education policies are sometimes perceived as ways of alleviating those concerns. How to assist veterans to readjust to civilian life? How to bolster American science so as to catch up to Soviet accomplishments symbolized by the launching of Sputnik? How to ease the depredations of poverty? How to respond to Supreme Court rulings that segregation is unconstitutional? These and numerous other challenges have regularly impelled presidents and their advisors to reckon with particular aspects of federal education policy, and each has given rise to identifiable federal programs. But in practically every instance, education has been a secondary concern—a passenger on some other issue making its way up the White House driveway. Unless that basic condition changes—that is, unless Washington asserts some primary responsibility for the well-being of the educational system *per se*, educators will continue to feel slighted by the president, save when they are able to hitch their concerns onto policy vehicles destined to drive up West Executive Avenue rather than to be parked in the nether reaches of the federal establishment.

While the Cat's Away . . .

Who looks after education for the president? How does the presidency deal with a large and intricate subject that seldom commands the personal attention of the chief executive? Three sets of people participate: presidential appointees scattered among the various agencies; officials at the Office of Management and Budget and other institutional units within the Executive Office of the President; and members of the president's own staff.

These three sets often intersect, sometimes in formal gatherings such as the working groups that met in Edward Morgan's office in 1969-70 and frequently through less clearly marked channels. Nevertheless, each retains its separate identity and perspective.

At the summit of every executive branch agency dwells a small cluster of presidential appointees, customarily members of the president's party and vulnerable to losing their jobs if the administration changes, if their performance displeases the president, or if it is decided that someone else has a better claim to their payroll slots. Only twenty or so "political appointees" inhabit HEW's Education Division, but dozens of others scattered around the government, from the cabinet down to barely visible staff assistants, influence aspects of federal education policy. Although all such appointees may, as a result of the terms of their employment, be thought to have the "president's interests" at heart, they do not necessarily have a presidential perspective on the matters within their domains. Those in the Education Division, for example, are apt to be educators, and thus to take an appropriately active interest in the well-being of their professional constituency. Most appointees also take a proprietary interest in the size of their agency's budget, in the reputation of its programs, and in the ways they are perceived in the press, in the Congress and within the peer groups to which they will probably return at the end of their service in Washington.

The Executive Office of the President encompasses several small agencies, of which the most prominent is the Office of Management and Budget. The staff of OMB, and that of other units such as the recently revived Office of Science and Technology Policy, blends political appointees and career government servants. Even the career men pride themselves on their "presidential perspective," however, and on their impartial professionalism.[3] Seldom do they find themselves accused of setting the interests of a particular agency, program, or outside interest group above those of the president, although when a "topical" unit such as the science office is created its employees must tread a fine line between the presidential perspective and that of interest groups who may view them as their champions. Because most policy issues have fiscal dimensions, the Office of Management and Budget ordinarily plays a prominent role in presidential education policy making, both through its own established routines—notably the preparation of the annual budget—and by providing information and advice to others making decisions. Indeed, many policy issues that ascend to the presidential level get completely resolved *within* the Office of Management and Budget, which does everything from "clearing" proposed legislation and congressional testimony to mediating disputes between agencies and monitoring the forms and procedures used in research studies and statistical compilations.

Finally, one must reckon with the president's own advisors, usually, if not very precisely, known as the "White House staff." Although most of its members do not physically sit inside the White House and although some are nominally on the payrolls of such quasi-agencies as the National Security Council and the Domestic Council, they customarily think of themselves as working directly for the man who occupies the Oval Office. Their jobs depend wholly on his, and their individual influence depends on how he uses them.[a] Occasionally one finds subject matter specialists on the president's staff, and it is not uncommon for individuals to be assigned as "liaisons" to particular interest groups or segments of the population. But the typical presidential aide is a generalist deemed

aThe White House has a permanent "support staff," of course, and some career government workers may temporarily serve there in professional capacities, particularly in the National Security Council, but in the main the professionals on the White House staff are political appointees.

competent to learn enough about the issues of the day to make decisions or render advice that will lead to their being handled in the way the president would presumably handle them if he were doing it himself.

As the issues coming to the White House have grown more numerous and complex and as the White House staff has grown apace, some differentiation and specialization has inevitably followed. One senior person may be given primary responsibility for domestic social policy, for example. His staff—for aides have deputies with assistants these days—might include someone charged with "human resource programs," and that person may assign one of his lieutenants to concentrate on education and related matters. Thus, within the lower echelons of the White House staff, there may emerge an education specialist who may or may not have a background in that field but who, in any case, is unlikely to enjoy direct access to the president or even to the inner circle of presidential assistants. Furthermore, his purview of federal education policy may be arbitrarily limited, since people in other sections of the staff will likely handle civil rights, "deregulation," scientific research, arts and humanities, and so forth. These portfolios are extremely difficult for anyone outside the White House to fathom, for they reflect many considerations, they tend to cut across agency, subject matter, and functional lines, and they change quite often.

From time to time, senior White House aides have surfaced as visible "education advisors." Douglass Cater is the most frequently cited example, although Daniel P. Moynihan played a kindred role in the early Nixon years. Educators watching the presidency naturally tend to focus on such people, in part because the rest of the White House operation seems so murky and impenetrable and in part, of course, because a senior advisor assigned to a particular subject is presumed to have great influence on policy.

These presidential aides walk a tight rope between specializing in a subject and advocating it. Delicate diplomacy is required, for it is practically a rule of thumb at the White House that the more pleased an interest group is with its access to the Oval Office via a trusted friend on the president's staff, the less pleased the president will be, and in time the access will diminish. It is reasonable for the president to want an advisor who can faithfully transmit the views of a particular constituency, check a program idea or policy proposal with that constituency, and serve as the president's legate at ceremonial and substantive gatherings of importance to the constituency. But if that advisor "goes native" and comes to regard himself, or to be seen by others, as the constituency's envoy to the White House rather than the administration's ambassador to the interest group, his usefulness to the president will be impaired and his influence correspondingly reduced.

The same advisor walks another difficult line between the virtue of a "visible presence" at the White House and the drawbacks of upstaging other presidential appointees whose titles suggest that they are in charge of particular subjects and are the administration's representatives to the pertinent interest groups.

Every policy realm that touches the White House also envelopes one or more agencies of the executive branch. The secretary of Health, Education and Welfare, for example, doubtless took that job with the understanding that he would be the president's senior advisor and main spokesman in matters of education policy. The assistant secretary for education and the commissioner of education can likewise glance at their walls and see the president's signature on documents that appear to invest them with primacy in the field of education. It is demeaning enough for them to know that their memoranda must detour across the desks of sundry HEW and White House aides before reaching the president—if in fact they ever do—and that their views are not the last word in administration policy making. But it is positively humiliating when a presidential assistant gets described in the press as the main gear in the education policy apparatus, when association representatives and university presidents seek audiences in the Executive Office Building rather than "across town," and when the Sunday television interviews feature White House staffers rather than themselves.

This problem reaches far beyond education, of course, for the tension between the ideal of "cabinet government" and the reality of White House staff influence touches the entire executive branch. Recent presidents have taken office with pious promises that the cabinet would be preeminent and have then continued to enlarge the size and the influence of the White House staff. There is much to be said for reversing this trend but to date no modern president has done so.[4] Hence, interest groups may be forgiven for scrutinizing the White House staff to see if they are apt to have friends at court.

In education policy, the absence of a cabinet department or independent agency further magnifies the symbolic importance of the White House staff. Whether powerful and respected, or weak and ignored, the secretary of HEW has much on his desk besides education, and some of his other concerns—notably health care and welfare policy—are at least equally tangled, demanding, and politically sensitive. Those officials within his sprawling domain who devote their full energies to education, primarily the assistant secretary, the commissioner, and their deputies, simply do not rank very high in the overall scheme of things within the executive branch and have no separate access to the president. Hence unless an "education advisor" is visibly situated within a hundred yards of the Oval Office, the education community has no reason to assume that anyone knowledgeable about its concerns, much less sympathetic to its interests, will play any role in presidential decisions that affect it.

There have been proposals from time to time to embed education in the permanent structure of the Executive Office of the President, such as through the creation of a Council of Education Advisors analogous to the Council of Economic Advisors. The idea is hardly novel, for many other interest groups have sought similar units to look after their favorite subjects. But presidents tend to eschew such proposals, not wanting to encumber themselves with specialized and institutionalized aides whose presence is apt to complicate the president's task whether he accepts or ignores their advice. Nixon did away with the Office of Science and Technology and handed the "science advisor" portfolio to the head of the National Science Foundation, but the hue and cry from aggrieved scientists and their allies in Congress led to restoration of the science office a few years later. If nothing else, this saga serves as a lesson to presidents that once a special interest unit is created, it is hard to get rid of it.

The creation of the Domestic Council shows an alternate approach, which is to aggregate many specialized subjects into larger staff units, where they can be evaluated and "traded off" alongside one another. The Domestic Council staff may harbor a number of specialists, including one who deals with education, but the context in which they work—a comprehensive unit presumed to have a presidential perspective on the entirety of domestic social policy—is very nearly the opposite of that implied by specialized staff units for particular subjects.

It is unlikely that this general approach to White House policy staffing will reverse or that education will obtain a permanent presidential advisor of its own. Even if it did, the president cannot be compelled to listen to him, and no one with the interests of the presidency at heart would seriously argue that the chief executive ought encumber himself with such an inflexible arrangement. It is one thing to say that presidents should be wise and secure enough to seek advice from many sources, to open their doors to varied interests, and to include on their personal staffs some individuals prepared to say things the president did not know or would just as soon not hear. But it is quite another to say that the White House should itself be made a microcosm of the nation, with every subject, every interest group, and every identifiable fraction of the population "represented" there. Big or small, specialized or full of generalists, the White House organization must remain flexible and idiosyncratic, able to change with the tastes and working style of each successive president, and able to adapt to unpredictable shifts in national and world affairs that command presidential attention.

Policy Modes

In education, as in other substantive domains, presidential policy making generally divides into three modes: the annual budget, day-to-day problem solving, and infrequent but thoroughgoing policy reviews keyed to the legislative calendar.

These processes have numerous links. Participants overlap. Fiscal, political, and philosophical considerations invest all three. A decision made in one context often affects those that can be made in the other two. But they differ, too, frequently in important ways.

The Budget

The president's annual budget submission represents the apex of more than a year's effort that starts at the program level of myriad federal agencies and slowly moves upward through the executive branch, where it culminates in a frantic autumn at the Office of Management and Budget and a number of appeals to, and decisions by, the president and his closest advisors. There is never enough money to satisfy all agency requests or interest group desires, and so successive stages of budget making consist of a series of ever-harder choices as the requests are whittled down.

Occasionally the budget provides a vehicle for new policy proposals, and often it contains half-veiled assumptions about legislative and programmatic changes that will be spelled out later in the year. Sometimes the president's annual budget message affords an opportunity to explain the philosophical underpinnings of the administration's approach to one or another large element of national life. But even more than other presidential policy modes, budget making is an incremental (and decremental) process, not a time for pathbreaking ideas about the conduct of government.[5] The budget is hewn out of existing laws, policies, and programs and is prepared by people whose primary assignment is to allot a limited amount of money to a near-limitless list of activities. This is policy making at its most elemental and its most sophisticated, and the result is a definitive statement of the administration's spending priorities. Many would term the annual budget the basic statement of presidential policy. But the very scope and urgency of budget assembly, which covers every program and agency every year, affords little leisure for a searching look at distinctive policy realms, and sweeping decisions made in that frenzied atmosphere may be ill-considered. That is why the otherwise attractive concept of "zero-based" budgeting will prove difficult to effect. To render their immense task manageable, budget examiners have to start with a great many assumptions about programs and policies. While they can expertly *apply* what they understand to be the administration's policy as made in other settings and at other times (and can, with equal skill, contribute to such policy reviews), the annual budget cycle presents them with few opportunities to ponder new ideas and to make nonincremental decisions. Also, the secrecy surrounding budget preparation virtually assures that any substantive changes will not have been reviewed with congressmen, interest groups, or possibly even senior officials of the line agencies. Instead, they typically originate with budget examiners whose premier responsibility is to guard expenditures, and they ordinarily get reviewed, if at all, by White House aides charged with gauging their political appeal rather than their merit. Budget making is an essential part of the process by which large spending priorities get determined, but when glossy new policies are forged in its heat, they may prove brittle and short-lived.

Fighting Fires

Problem solving or "fire fighting" is what most White House aides would say they spend most of their time doing. Oftentimes the blaze is nothing more than a flicker: A letter to the President that needs a reply drafted, a speech to be prepared, an agency official who wants to talk about something, appointments to an advisory commission, a proclamation. Sometimes, however, a vast swath of governmental hillside may seem to be aflame: A well-publicized and controversial piece of legislation demands a presidential signature or veto, a scandal surfaces in a large federal program, a major national organization denounces the president's handling of its interests, a cabinet member loudly protests the position he is asked to take in testifying before a congressional committee. Domestic advisors have no "situation room" where the lights shine all night when disorder engulfs some distant part of the globe, but plenty of problems arrive at the White House every day, and solving them on the president's behalf—or preparing a solution for his scrutiny—consumes vast amounts of staff time.

It probably consumes too much. As often as not, the fire could be quenched at the agency level, and the only reason the White House hoses are unrolled is because the agency is too timid, because the presidential staff is too large to keep fully occupied on truly presidential matters, and because of the decades-old tendency for more and more solutions to smaller and smaller problems to be worked out at the pinnacle of the executive branch. Certainly more "policy" could get made, and more seat-of-the-pants solutions avoided, if the White House staff bucked ordinary problems down to the agencies, where a cadre of presidential appointees is available to take them on, and if the president's own aides kept their gaze focused on the large policy choices that, once made, give needed direction to the "problem solvers."

Many decisions get made while fighting fires, but as in the budget review, this mode of staff activity does not lend itself to the creation of policy so much as to its application. The aide charged with solving a particular problem can do so most simply, speedily, and with least fear of being reversed if he can locate an extant policy or precedent that he can apply to the instant situation. His task is easiest if he can draw on something the president previously said or signed. Depending on the nature of the problem and the aide's own stature or perhaps his courage, he will have some latitude to refine, embellish, or extend the precedent. If he cannot find one, he may fall back on expressions of general administration philosophy, he may consult with other staffers, he may seek the advice of the cognizant agency (quite a different matter than an assistant secretary calling the White House for ratification of a solution that the agency devised) and, *in extremis*, he may contrive to obtain the president's own views. But the fundamental point stands: "Fire fighting" does not lend itself to searching policy review, to bursts of creativity, or to major new initiatives.

The Quadrennial Review

These reviews are reserved for the third mode of presidential policy making—in an important sense the only one that warrants the designation—namely the periodic, systematic examination of federal policy in a particular realm of government activity, such as was undertaken by the two education working groups of 1969-70.

This is not a random or trivial event, and it is closely linked to the election of a new president and the arrival in Washington of a new administration. Besides being fresh, full of enthusiasm, and eager to put its own stamp on national affairs, the new team arrives with a bundle of ideas and commitments: the pledges the president made during his campaign, the platform adopted at his party's convention, at least four years' accumulated criticisms of the policies of the outgoing officials, and the pet notions and preferred remedies of their successors. Basking in the mandate of the election just past, they are not yet consumed by the demands of the campaign that will commence two and a half years in the future. The public awaits evidence of what the new administration has in mind. A thousand interest groups anxiously look for earnests of its intentions toward them. The press and the Congress traditionally grant the occupant of the Oval Office at least a brief "honeymoon" before they start disputing him. It is the ineluctable task of the fledgling presidency to take up one and then another policy domain, to analyze what the government is already doing there, to settle upon the goals and ideas that will animate future legislative and administrative efforts, to weave those ideas into a comprehensible philosophy, and to rank them according to their importance.

Basic policy must be shaped with some dispatch, because other modes of presidential activity—budget preparation, "fire fighting," and the rest—all depend on it. Until it is clear what the president thinks about a subject and what general posture his administration is going to adopt, those who work for him have no anchor for the many subordinate decisions they are called upon to make.

Hence the early months of a new president's term are a tumult of policy-making. As Moynihan warned his future staff colleagues during a preinaugural discussion at the Hotel Pierre, "If you cannot do what you set out to do in the first couple of years, forget it."[6] Perversely, however, the early months may also find the presidency ill equipped to make such large and lasting determinations about complex national affairs. Appointees in the White House and the agencies have barely located the water cooler, chosen their aides, and begun to get acquainted with each other. Many know little about the programs over which they preside, save whatever impressions they brought with them to Washington. Campaign speeches provide the only substantial fund of clues to what the president himself thinks, and hundreds of the decisions they must make involve issues that he may never have addressed. Relationships with

Congress and interest groups are still tentative. The fiscal implications of various policy options are hard to fathom.

Yet there will seldom be a second chance. The presidency has neither time nor capacity constantly to reexamine basic policy directions. With a thousand subjects demanding attention, only a few can receive it more than once in a four year term, and if the president is reelected, it is not uncommon for eight years to elapse before the next systematic review. In a field such as education, Congress contributes to this infrequency, for its committees are busy, too, and the programs it enacts are generally authorized for three to five years at a time. Moreover, once the president's policy is determined, strong forces discourage him from reexamining it: Hundreds of related decisions begin to be made throughout the executive branch, ranging from billion dollar budget choices down to the phrasing of replies to schoolchildren's letters. Because these decisions are keyed to the administration's policy, in time they add considerable momentum to that policy, such that altering it demands more presidential energy than was required to make it in the first place. No administration wishes to appear fickle or erratic, and by the middle of the term, its policy, whatever it is, will have been clearly identified with the president, will have helped shape others' impressions of him, and will have had whatever effect it is going to have on his future political prospects. His honeymoon with Congress, the press, and the interest groups will long since have ended, and his advisors will have turned their own attention to the forthcoming campaign. While they still have to quench numerous brushfires—often ignited by sparks from the initial policy review—they have no time or inclination to rethink their assumptions or reformulate the president's stated goals. Their subsequent statements and proposals, such as the second round of education messages that Nixon sent Congress in 1971, are apt to be modifications of earlier versions, not brand new ideas.

As one of the leading responsibilities of the presidency, therefore, the quadrennial review is both predictable and extraordinary: It is bound to happen once and unlikely to happen twice, at least in a single policy domain. Hence the ways in which the president and his advisors set about it deserve careful scrutiny.

If one assumes that the chief executive has neither the time nor the inclination to carry out his own reviews singlehandedly, it follows that he must obtain help, and it is likely that he will initially reach out for that help to the familiar sources: his own staff, the other units of the Executive Office, and his appointees in the line agencies. Whatever mechanisms he establishes to carry out the quadrennial review on his behalf, we can assume he starts with three requirements.

First, the person or persons put in charge of policy development must be loyal to him and have the interests of his administration at heart. Because they will be acting as extensions of him, they must share his perspective, understand his convictions, and care about his reputation and political fate.

Second, a number of people must participate. In a complex policy domain such as education that is laden with dozens of existing federal programs run by multiple agencies and with subtle political alignments, potentially high budget costs, and hazy social science findings, no prudent president would rely on the views of a single person, however capable or trustworthy. Particularly in the early days of the term, when many of his advisors are new to him, new to Washington, new to the issues they are given charge of, and new to each other as well, policy development calls for a group process. Moreover, regardless of subject area, the preparation of a presidential message and its supporting materials is a large undertaking that can only be done expeditiously if many steps are carried out at the same time and if the several sequences are carefully synchronized. Clearly, a team effort is required.

Third, the policy review of a particular subject area must be meshed with others in related areas and with overarching considerations such as the administration's general philosophy, its budget priorities, and political objectives. Whether the immediate topic is higher education, mass transit, or health care, the president is not well served if his advisors work in a vacuum, isolated from the hundred and one variables—many of them bearing little evident relationship to the issue at hand—that he cannot disregard. Even if he has no blueprint clearly in mind, his election campaign stressed certain themes and in time his administration will begin to display a grand design that will strongly influence his future prospects at the polls and his place in the history books. Each major policy statement must contribute to, at least not detract from, the coherence of that design.

Is a Working Group Inevitable?

While the general requirements sketched above do circumscribe the president's choice of a policy development mechanism, they do not dictate any particular format. Over the years, presidents have settled on different strategems for reviewing federal activities in education and other subjects and for shaping new proposals. The process may be orderly, sequential, and unitary, or it may be multifaceted, simultaneous, and complex. It may include trusted confidants, loyal appointees, career government officials, or outsiders. It may involve the president heavily or sparingly. It may strive for consensus-in-advance from as many affected parties as possible, or it may work toward a bold statement of high intellectual integrity.

Certainly no president is obliged to follow the policy development format of the working group that characterized the early Nixon administration. Indeed, five defining attributes of the Morgan working groups need not obtain at all. Although the president pays a price for each one that he discards, he also gains something in return.

First, it does not have to be a formally constituted group at all. Although the process must be organized and must involve a number of participants, the president is not obliged to put a single person in charge nor are his designees required to form themselves into a cohesive task force with a defined membership. One team may be put to work on some aspects of the subject, while individual persons are entrusted with others. Policy proposals eventually tied together in a single Message to Congress may be prepared by advisors who never discuss them with each other and who use radically different procedures to develop them. Only the president and, perhaps, a speechwriter, need be familiar with all the message's elements prior to its delivery. To be sure, a loosely woven process invites snags. Agencies affected by a particular proposal and advisors interested in it may not know about it and thus not have the opportunity to influence it. If sufficiently vexed, they may lobby against it or quietly fail to carry it out. Policies emanating from multiple sources may turn out to clash in philosophy or in practice, and the sum of their parts may be costlier, less effective, or more troublesome politically than the products of a single task force. Moreover, if not designating a formal working group means the process has no leader or clear-cut structure for making decisions and resolving disputes, then the president must invest more of his own energies in coordination and direction. That he may not wish or have the time to do.

Second, policy development need not be centered in the White House, even if it surely terminates there. It is entirely possible for the president to designate a member of his cabinet or sub-cabinet as his agent, and for proposals destined for the Oval Office not even to reach the White House until they are virtually complete. Although the president may reserve to his personal staff the actual crafting of language for Messages to Congress and other documents that implicate him directly, there is no intrinsic reason why program analyses must be conducted or fresh policy ideas generated within the White House complex, and his staff has few inherent advantages in this regard. Indeed, there is much to be said for relying on those who live with the programs, the interest groups, and the cognizant congressional committees to devise timely and feasible initiatives. In entrusting the process to cabinet officers or others outside his immediate circle, however, the president takes several risks, and these may be especially keen in a subject such as education which has no cabinet-level agency of its own.[7] Since a number of departments are sure to have an interest in any policy departures bold enough to warrant a presidential message, an interagency perspective is essential. But officials outside the White House, even if they are cabinet members, cannot easily "pull rank" on their peers from other departments. Battles over agency turf and bureaucratic self-interest may blur the equally essential presidential perspective and sap the vigor of the ideas themselves. Similarly, those responsible for running programs and looking after the welfare of particular federal units may not fully comprehend the philosophical or political dynamics of the presidency, and their instinctive appetite for more funds may dull their sensitivity to overall budget priorities.

Third, the policy development process need not be confined to the presidency—that is, to political appointees in the executive branch of the national government. It can and ordinarily should include many who do not belong to the president's entourage: career officials who are intimately familiar with the strengths and weaknesses of present programs, with the half-veiled sensitivities of congressional subcommittees, and with the desires and flashpoints of key interest groups; leaders of the Senate and the House, committee chairmen, ranking minority members and Capitol Hill staff members on whose combined response will hinge the fate of the president's legislative proposals; disinterested experts who have studied a particular subject for years and who know more about it than even the ablest of presidential appointees can hope to learn in four years in Washington; lobbyists and executives of the various national associations that comprise the primary constituency for the policies under review; pundits whose reaction to the president's proposals will define the terms for whatever national debate occurs on them; and ordinary citizens whose views, however ill informed, may signal the concerns of the ultimate constituency, the electorate.

As we have seen, the president has at his disposal a hundred different means of obtaining advice from outsiders, ranging from quiet conversations to massive White House conferences, and invariably at least some views of some outsiders seep into the policy-making process. Purposely gathering many such opinions has clear-cut virtues ranging from the excellence of an idea obtained thereby to the political advantage gained by neutralizing (or coopting) potential critics in advance. But the drawbacks cannot be ignored: If the subject is at all controversial and resources are at all limited—both conditions being more the norm than the exception in presidential policy making—perfect consensus is unobtainable, and the more people consulted, the more elusive even partial agreement may prove. Broad participation can lead to policy stalemate. It always leads to delay. It often exposes the president to critical publicity before he has made up his mind. And it may siphon far more time and attention than he can afford into mediating, placating, meeting with, hearing out, and thanking his external advisors only to find himself assaulted the next day by yet another group whose views were overlooked.

Fourth, the policy development process need not restrict the president to a single channel of information and opinion. Indeed, most serious students of the presidency contend that it should not, that he is better served by—and should demand—a variety of ideas and advice from disparate sources. Even though a conscientious working group, such as those chaired by Edward L. Morgan, may take pains to present the president with choices, to accompany its options with clearly stated pros and cons, and to expose him to its own differences of opinion, it cannot transcend its built-in limitations. From its inception, the main task of a working group is to whittle down its policy domain to manageable size: defining the problems in one set of terms; excluding some issues and highlighting others; accepting constraints of budget, timing, and ideology; mixing its analyses with political calculations; postulating that extant federal programs be kept or scrapped. The group's usefulness is bounded on one side by the combined knowledge and predilections of its individual members and, on the other, by the elemental dynamics of any group that is expected to produce some sort of agreement.[8] Hence a president is wise to consult with others, too, to obtain information and advice from several sources and to expose the policies urged by one group to the criticism of others. But again, when he complicates the process he complicates his own task. If he does not delegate the job of "pulling it all together" to some individual or task force, he must do it by himself and that may lead to unmanageable demands on his time and temper. For one of a president's most difficult challenges is to ration himself and not let any single policy domain, no matter how interesting, keep him from paying adequate attention to a thousand others.

Finally, the policy development process need not adopt the Nixon penchant for surprise. Implicit in the four previous observations is the idea that presidential policy making, at least in domestic affairs, does not have to be a covert operation conducted exclusively by loyalists, with its product suddenly displayed before the widened eyes of an unsuspecting (but perhaps now needlessly suspicious) public. To be sure, even the most secretive of presidents cannot keep the shades drawn all the time, and the proposals of the Morgan working groups were neither revolutionary in their content nor all that startling when publicly presented in March 1970. Nor is there any reason to suppose that they would have been markedly different if their advance exposure had taken the form of widespread consultations rather than random leaks. The working groups knew fairly early what they wanted the president to say and took some justifiable pride in their forthrightness in urging upon him policies that they knew to be correct, albeit ill appreciated. They were not willfully secretive so much as simply amenable to the president's preferred manner of staging his policy announcements, which was with all the trappings of a grand unveiling. Yet at least in education policy, nothing was gained by stealth, and as the later years of the Nixon administration showed all too clearly, much may be lost when the presidency keeps its activities to itself.

At the same time, one wants to guard against inflating the value of openness *per se*. While it is unquestionably an attractive characteristic for the presidency in general, it does not necessarily make for better policy. Indeed, there is some reason to suspect that when "sunshine" rules are applied to policy development in its germinal stage, they foster caution, incrementalism, and a greater concern for the desires of those watching than for the interests of the public.

Settling on a Process

We have established that the quadrennial review does not have to ape the working group style of the early Nixon years. But we have also concluded that the president needs a complex mechanism of some design to assist him in carrying out many such reviews simultaneously. How, then, does he find the format that suits him?

He may not find it at once, or stick with the one he first tries. Even the Nixon White House recalibrated its domestic policy machinery several times, from the creative hubbub of the Urban Affairs Council in 1969, to the Ehrlichman working groups of 1970, to the more formal Domestic Council thereafter.

In part, the shape of the policy development process reflects the president's personal style. Does he like boisterous participatory sessions where conflicting ideas are aired, where many people know what he's considering, and where his decisions are thus exposed? Has he the time and temperament to deal with a lot of different people on a single subject? Or does he favor neatness and order, the ability to take a single document that is the distillation of many ideas and the synthesis of many opinions, and retreat to contemplate it at his leisure and make his decisions in private? It is because presidents differ and because organizational patterns and practices that serve one admirably may be intolerable to his successor that Stephen Hess and other scholars urge the greatest possible flexibility in the overall structure of the presidency.[9]

In part, the policy development blueprint also changes with the subject at hand, with the president's attitude toward that subject, and with the capacity of others to handle it for him. Education, as we have seen, holds scant interest for most presidents, and they are therefore apt to entrust it to a mechanism that calls for minimal personal involvement. At the same time, since education touches so many departments and since it lacks a cabinet member of its own, there is some reason to lodge the policy development process at the White House, close to the former professors who surround the president and distant from the suspect professionals who inhabit the Office of Education and other line agencies.

In part, however, the nature of the quadrennial review of education and other policy domains also reflects the chief executive's overall approach to his office. A president striving to run a "collegial presidency," in which policy development is entrusted to his cabinet members and other lieutenants in the line agencies and in which only the toughest political choices reach his own desk, would likely permit the secretary of HEW to take the lead in education policy making for the entire administration. The White House staff would have little to do with the process. No presidential aide would succeed an Edward L. Morgan as chairman of the education working groups.

If instead the president presided over an "administrative presidency," there still would be scant likelihood of a complex, semiparticipatory policy process based in the White House.[10] Indeed, the process might not emphasize Messages to Congress and new legislation at all, but rather executive and managerial actions intended to carry out the president's ideas with little reference to structure and statute.

The White House working groups as developed under Nixon bore some characteristics of what Schlesinger branded the "Imperial Presidency."[11] These included a general disregard for Congress, bureaucrats and interest groups alike; the concentration of decisions in a swollen White House staff; an impulse (manifest in the stress laid on the rhetoric of the policy messages) to reach over the traditional structures of government and appeal directly to "Everyman"; and a tendency to channel the president's information to him through a single network of trusted aides, protect him from exposure to situations where he might be vulnerable, and keep both contrary ideas and contrary people at a safe distance.

Yet the working group mode has important virtues, too, and it is not surprising that one chief executive after another has adopted some variation on it to shape presidential policy, particularly in the early months of a new administration. It displays many elements of traditional "good government" doctrine by promoting comprehensiveness, rationality, cool contemplation of alternatives and clear-cut decisions, while rationing the president's own time and energies. Its participatory character serves to enmesh all the interested units of the executive branch in decisions so that their views are noted and so that, once the President fixes upon a course of action, their cooperation is assured.

The quadrennial review is an important event that demands deliberateness and a certain distance from the hurly-burly of daily emergencies and agency self-interests. Whereas most other processes within the executive branch are well handled in a hierarchical, bureaucratic mode, a serious attempt to shape basic policy alternatives and recommendations for the president calls for quite a different governmental style. Decision making within an agency puts a premium on consistency and uniformity and it promotes efficiency by obliging each official to share with others only those decisions he cannot make by himself within accepted norms and procedures. But policy development at the level of the presidency is better undertaken by a task force of trusted appointees who are physically removed from their executive responsibilities, intellectually liberated from the "chain of command," and instructed to bring their best ideas and shrewdest judgment to bear on the great affairs of the nation. In this effort, they are apt to function well in a "seminar" format such as that provided by the working group, where they can learn from one another, where each can supply his own distinctive blend of knowledge and perspective, where unconventional ideas can be explored and familar assumptions challenged, and where the quality of a person's thinking and the persuasiveness of his presentation count for more than his rank in the hierarchy. The efficiency provided by a working group lies in its singular ability to concentrate energies and intellects rather than to diffuse them. In addition, the working group mode is well suited to fostering speed, orderliness, and confidentiality in policy making. While those may not be the noblest values to be held at the summit of American national government, they are undeniably appealing to the people there, not least to the president himself, and therefore not to be lightly surrendered, even if each also has its costs.

Who, then, advises the president on education policy, and how do they go about it? The only honest answer is whomever he wants and howsoever he wants them to. The Constitution is silent. No statute is binding. No structure can compel him to listen, let alone to concur, except when he is so inclined. In the last analysis, presidential policy reflects the values, ideas, and priorities of the chief executive and those around him. It can be no better or wiser than the president and the people he selects to handle it for him. All one can ask of structure and process is that it bring out and enhance the best in them.

Appendixes

Appendix A
Special Message to the
Congress on Education
Reform, March 3, 1970

To the Congress of the United States:
American education is in urgent need of reform.

A nation justly proud of the dedicated efforts of its millions of teachers and educators must join them in a searching re-examination of our entire approach to learning.

We must stop thinking of primary and secondary education as the school system alone—when we now have reason to believe that young people may be learning much more *outside* school than they learn in school.

We must stop imagining that the Federal government had a cohesive education policy during a period of explosive expansion—when our Federal education programs are largely fragmented and disjointed, and too often administered in a way that frustrates local and private efforts.

We must stop letting wishes color our judgments about the educational effectiveness of many special compensatory programs, when—despite some dramatic and encouraging exceptions—there is growing evidence that most of them are not yet measurably improving the success of poor children in school.

We must stop pretending that we understand the mystery of the learning process, or that we are significantly applying science and technology to the techniques of teaching—when we spend less than one half of one percent of our educational budget on research, compared with 5% of our health budget and 10% of defense.

We must stop congratulating ourselves for spending nearly as much money on education as does the entire rest of the world—$65 billion a year on all levels—when we are not getting as much as we should out of the dollars we spend.

A new reality in American education can mark the beginning of an era of reform and progress for those who teach and those who learn. Our schools have served us nobly for centuries; to carry that tradition forward, the decade of the 1970s calls for thoughtful redirection to improve our ability to make up for environmental deficiencies among the poor; for long-range provisions for financial support of schools; for more efficient use of the dollars spent on education; for structural reforms to accommodate new discoveries; and for the enhancement of learning before and beyond the school.

When educators, school boards and government officials alike admit that we have a great deal to learn about the way we teach, we will begin to climb the up staircase toward genuine reform.

Therefore, *I propose that the Congress create a National Institute of Education* as a focus for educational research and experimentation in the United States. When fully developed, the Institute would be an important element in the nation's educational system, overseeing the annual expenditure of as much as a quarter of a billion dollars.

I am establishing a President's Commission on School Finance to help States and communities to analyze the fiscal plight of their public and non-public schools. We must make the nation aware of the dilemmas our schools face, new methods of organization and finance must be found, and public and non-public schools should together begin to chart the fiscal course of their educational planning for the Seventies.

I propose new steps to help States and communities to achieve the Right to Read for every young American. I will shortly request that funds totalling $200 million be devoted to this objective during fiscal 1971. The basic ability to read is a right that should be denied to no one, and the pleasures found in books and libraries should be available to all.

I propose that the Department of Health, Education, and Welfare and the Office of Economic Opportunity begin now to establish a network of child development projects to improve our programs devoted to the first five years of life. In fiscal 1971, a minimum of $52 million will be provided for this purpose.

New Measurements of Achievement

What makes a "good" school? The old answer was a school that maintained high standards of plant and equipment; that had a reasonable number of children per classroom; whose teachers had good college and often graduate training; a school that kept up to date with new curriculum developments, and was alert to new techniques in instruction. This was a fair enough definition so long as it was assumed that there was a direct connection between these "school characteristics" and the actual amount of learning that takes place in a school.

Years of educational research, culminating in the Equal Educational Opportunity Survey of 1966 have, however, demonstrated that this direct, uncomplicated relationship does not exist.

Apart from the general public interest in providing teachers an honorable and well-paid professional career, there is only one important question to be asked about education: *What do the children learn?*

Unfortunately, it is simply not possible to make any confident deduction from school characteristics as to what will be happening to the children in any particular school. Fine new buildings alone do not predict high achievement. Pupil-teacher ratios may not make as much difference as we used to think. Expensive equipment may not make as much difference as its salesmen would have us believe.

And yet we know that something does make a difference.

The *outcome* of schooling—what children learn—is profoundly different for different groups of children and different parts of the country. Although we do not seem to understand just what it is in one school or school system that produces a different outcome from another, one conclusion is inescapable: *We do not yet have equal educational opportunity in America.*

The purpose of the National Institute of Education would be to begin the serious, systematic search for new knowledge needed to make educational opportunity truly equal.

The corresponding need in the school systems of the nation is to begin the responsible, open measurement of how well the educational process is working. It matters very little how much a school building costs; it matters a great deal how much a child in that building learns. An important beginning in measuring the end result of education has already been made through the National Assessment of Educational Progress being conducted by the Education Commission of the States.

To achieve this fundamental reform it will be necessary to develop broader and more sensitive measurements of learning than we now have.

The National Institute of Education would take the lead in developing these new measurements of educational output. In doing so it should pay as much heed to what are called the "immeasurables" of schooling (largely because no one has yet learned to measure them) such as responsibility, wit and humanity as it does to verbal and mathematical achievement.

In developing these new measurements, we will want to begin by comparing the actual educational effectiveness of schools in similar economic and geographic circumstances. We will want to be alert to the fact that in our present educational system we will often find our most devoted, most talented, hardest working teachers in those very schools where the general level of achievement is lowest. They are often there because their commitment to their profession sends them where the demands upon their profession are the greatest.

From these considerations we derive another new concept: *accountability*. School administrators and school teachers alike are responsible for their performance, and it is in their interest as well as in the interest of their pupils that they be held accountable. Success should be measured not by some fixed national norm, but rather by the results achieved in relation to the actual situation of the particular school and the particular set of pupils.

For years the fear of "national standards" has been one of the bugaboos of education. There has never been any serious effort to impose national standards on educational programs, and if we act wisely in this generation we can be reasonably confident that no such effort will arise in future generations. The problem is that in opposing some mythical threat of "national standards" what we have too often been doing is avoiding accountability for our own local performance. We have, as a nation, too long avoided thinking of the *productivity* of schools.

This is a mistake because it undermines the principle of local control of education. Ironic though it is, the avoidance of accountability is the single most serious threat to a continued, and even more pluralistic educational system. Unless the local community can obtain dependable measures of just how well its school system is performing for its children, the demand for national standards will become even greater and in the end almost certainly will prevail. When local officials do not respond to a real local need, the search begins for a level of officialdom that will do so, and all too often in the past this search has ended in Washington.

I am determined to see to it that the flow of power in education goes toward, and not away from, the local community. The diversity and freedom of education in this nation, founded on local administration and State responsibility, must prevail.

The National Institute of Education

As the first step toward reform, we need a coherent approach to research and experimentation. Local schools need an objective national body to evaluate new departures in teaching that are being conducted here and abroad and a means of disseminating information about projects that show promise.

The National Institute of Education would be located in the Department of Health, Education, and Welfare under the Assistant Secretary for Education, with a permanent staff of outstanding scholars from such disciplines as psychology, biology and the social sciences, as well as education.

While it would conduct basic and applied educational research itself, the National Institute of Education would conduct a major portion of its research by contract with universities, non-profit institutions and other organizations. Ultimately, related research activities of the Office of Education would be transferred to the Institute.

It would have a National Advisory Council of distinguished scientists, educators and laymen to ensure that educational research in the Institute achieves a high level of sophistication, rigor and efficiency.

The Institute would set priorities for research and experimentation projects and vigorously monitor the work of its contractors to ensure a useful research product.

It would develop criteria and measures for enabling localities to assess educational achievement and for evaluating particular educational programs, and would provide technical assistance to State and local agencies seeking to evaluate their own programs.

It would also link the educational research and experimentation of other Federal agencies—the Office of Economic Opportunity, the Department of Labor, the Department of Defense, the National Science Foundation and others—to the attainment of particular national educational goals.

Here are a few of the areas the National Institute of Education would explore:

(a) *Compensatory Education.* The most glaring shortcoming in American education today continues to be the lag in essential learning skills in large numbers of children of poor families.

In the last decade, the Government launched a series of ambitious, idealistic, and costly programs for the disadvantaged, based on the assumption that extra resources would equalize learning opportunity and eventually help eliminate poverty.

In some instances, such programs have dramatically improved children's educational achievement. In many cases, the programs have provided important auxiliary services such as medical care and improved nutrition. They may also have helped prevent some children from falling even further behind.

However, the best available evidence indicates that most of the compensatory education programs have not measurably helped poor children catch up.

Recent findings on the two largest such programs are particularly disturbing. We now spend more than $1 billion a year for educational programs run under Title I of the Elementary and Secondary Education Act. Most of these have stressed the teaching of reading, but before-and-after tests suggest that only 19% of the children in such programs improve their reading significantly; 13% appear to fall behind more than expected; and more than two-thirds of the children remain unaffected—that is, they continue to fall behind. In our Headstart program, where so much hope is invested, we find that youngsters enrolled only for the summer achieve almost no gains, and the gains of those in the program for a full year are soon matched by their non-Headstart classmates from similarly poor backgrounds.

Thoughtful men recognize the limitations of such measurements and would not conclude that the programs thus assessed are without value. It may be necessary to wait many years before the full impact of such programs on the lives of poor youngsters can be ascertained. But as we continue to conduct special compensatory education for the disadvantaged, we must recognize that our present knowledge about how to overcome poor backgrounds is so limited that major expansion of such programs could not be confidently based on their results.

While our understanding of what works in compensatory education is still inadequate, we do know that the social and economic environment which surrounds a child at home and outside of school probably has more effect on what he learns than the quality of the school he now attends. Therefore, the major expansion of income support proposed in the Family Assistance Plan should also have an important educational effect.

The first order of business of the National Institute of Education would be to determine what is needed—inside and outside of school—to make our compensatory education effort successful. To help get this process under way now, I have also reactivated the National Advisory Council on the Education of Disadvantaged Children, and have appointed a slate of distinguished educators who will make recommendations and help monitor our efforts in this field. The nation cannot afford defeat in this area.

(b) *The Right To Read.* In September, the nation's chief education officer, Dr. James E. Allen, Jr., proclaimed the Right to Read as a goal for the 1970's. I endorse this goal.

Achievement of the Right to Read will require a national effort to develop new curricula and to better apply the many methods and programs that already exist. Where we do not know how to solve a reading problem, the National Institute of Education would undertake the research. But often we find that someone does know how, and the Institute would make that knowledge available in forms that can be adopted by local schools.

In some critical areas, we already know how to work toward achieving the Right to Read for our nation's children. In the coming year, I will ask the Congress to appropriate substantial resources for two programs that can most readily serve to achieve this new commitment—the program that assists school libraries to obtain books, and the program that provides funds through the states for special education improvement projects.

I will shortly ask Congress to increase the funds for these two programs— funds which are available to public and nonpublic schools alike—to $200 million. I shall direct the Commissioner of Education to work with State and local officials to assist them in using these programs to teach children to read. This is a purpose which I believe to be of the very highest priority for our schools, and a right which, with the cooperation of the nation's educators, can be achieved for every young American.

(c) *Television and Learning.* Most education takes place outside the school. Although we often mistakenly equate "schooling" with "learning," we should begin to pay far greater attention to what youngsters learn during the more than three quarters of their time they spend elsewhere.

In the last twenty years, there has been a revolution in the way most boys and girls—and their parents—occupy themselves. The average high school student, for example, by the time he graduates, has spent 11,000 hours in school—and 15,000 hours watching television.

Our goal must be to increase the use of the television medium and other technological advances to stimulate the desire to learn and to help teach.

The technology is here, but we have not yet learned how to employ it to our full advantage. How can local school systems extend and support their curricula working with local television stations? How can new techniques of programmed learning be applied so as to make each television set an effective teaching aid? How can television, audiovisual aids, the telephone, and the availability of computer libraries be combined to form a learning unit in the home, revolutionizing "homework" by turning a chore into an adventure in learning?

The National Institute of Education would examine questions such as these, especially in that vital area where out-of-school activities can combine with modern technology and public policy to enhance our children's education. It will work in concert with other organizations and agencies dedicated to the educational uses of television technology. Prominent among these is the Corporation for Public Broadcasting, which the Congress established in 1967 as a private entity to channel and shape the use of Federal funds in support of public broadcasting. With its authorization for Federal funds expiring shortly, the time has come to extend the Federal support for the Corporation to stimulate its continuing growth and improvement. Accordingly, the Secretary of Health, Education, and Welfare is today transmitting a bill to authorize funds for the Corporation for a three-year period. This will permit the Corporation to grow in the orderly and planned way so important to a new undertaking. A portion of the annual Federal funding would be based on matching the dollars raised by the Corporation from non-Federal sources. The Congress did not intend that the Corporation derive its funds solely from the Federal Government. Therefore, increased contributions from private sources should be stimulated during the early years through the incentive offered in the matching process.

(d) *Experimental Schools.* As a bridge between basic educational research and actual school practices, I consider the Experimental Schools program to be highly important. Accordingly, I renew my request to the Congress to appropriate the full amount asked—$25 million in Fiscal Year 1971.

The Secretary of Health, Education, and Welfare is today transmitting a bill to establish the National Institute of Education. We have taken a similar approach in biomedical research through the National Institutes of Health; this effort in education would be an historic step forward.

The President's Commission on School Finance

I am today signing an Executive Order [11513] establishing a President's Commission on School Finance, to be in existence for two years, reporting to the President periodically on future revenue needs and fiscal priorities for public and non-public schools.

(a) *From Quantity to Quality.* Over the past twenty years the public schools have experienced the greatest expansion in their history. Enrollments increased by 80%—from 25 million to 45 million pupils—in those two decades.

But now the period of steep enrollment growth in the schools is over: The birthrate has been declining for about ten years and the number of pupils in the public schools is expected to rise only slightly in the decade ahead. This means that the schools, no longer faced with a problem of sharply increasing numbers, will now be able to concentrate on finding improved educational methods. They can now shift their emphasis from quantity to quality.

(b) *Future Financial Needs.* Despite this leveling-off of enrollments, additional resources will be necessary, particularly if the present rate of growth in *per pupil* expenditures continues. Yet, because we have neglected to plan how we will deal with school finance, we have great instability and uncertainty in the financial structure of education.

(c) *Disparity Among Districts and States.* The continuing if narrowing gap in educational expenditures between rich and poor States and rich and poor school districts is cause for national concern. Differences in dollars per pupil are not in themselves wrong; in a democracy, communities should have the right to provide extra support to their schools if they wish. But some areas with a low tax base find it difficult or impossible to provide *adequate* support to their schools, a problem that crosses State lines in an era of mobility—when the poorly taught of one area frequently become unemployed adults elsewhere.

The need is apparent for a central body to study the different approaches being pioneered by States and local districts, and to disseminate the information about successes achieved and problems encountered at the local level.

(d) *Sources of Funds for Education.* State support accounts for 38% of school revenues, Federal support for about 8%, with 54% of the burden carried locally. Of the local funds, almost all come from property taxes, but that tax base is not keeping up with educational expenditures. A major review of the tax resources and needs of education is in order.

The best method of providing direct Federal monetary aid to education, and the one most consistent with local control of education, is through the system of revenue sharing which I proposed to the Congress in August. Much of the tax revenue which the Federal government would return to the States will probably be used where two-fifths of State and local funds now go—to the schools. Revenue sharing proposals which would total five billion dollars annually by 1975 will help States and localities meet their educational and other needs in the way that ensures the most diversity and the most responsiveness to local need—without Federal domination.

A related and important reform is urgently needed in the present program of grants to schools in Federally-impacted areas. As presently constituted, this program neither assists States to determine their own education expenditures nor redirects funds to the individual districts in greatest need. That is why, in the Federal Economy Act submitted to the Congress last week, I called for a thoroughgoing reform of this program. The President's Commission on School Finance will examine the combined effects of this reform, the potential of revenue sharing for educational finance, and the impact of savings accruing to States under the proposed Family Assistance Program, and will assist State and Federal agencies to plan effectively for these important changes.

(e) *Possible Efficiencies.* Many public and non-public school systems make inefficient use of their facilities and staff. The nine-month school year may have been justified when most youngsters helped in the fields during the summer months, but it is doubtful whether many communities can any longer afford to let expensive facilities sit idle for one-quarter of the year.

Thousands of small school districts—some without schools—continue to exist, resulting in inequities in both finance and education. On the other hand, some of our large city school systems have become too large, too bureaucratic, and insensitive to varying educational needs.

The present system of Federal grants frequently creates inefficiency. There are now about 40 different Federal categorical grant programs in elementary and secondary education. This system of carving up Federal aid to education into a series of distinct programs may have adverse educational effects. Federal "pieces" do not add up to the whole of education and they may distract the attention of educators away from the big picture and into a constant scramble for special purpose grants. Partly for this reason, I will continue to recommend to the Congress plans for consolidation of grants into packages that are truly useful to States and localities receiving them. This would place much more administrative control of these Federal funds in local hands, removing red tape and providing flexibility.

(f) *Non-Public Schools.* The non-public elementary and secondary schools in the United States have long been an integral part of the nation's educational establishment—supplementing in an important way the main task of our public school system. The non-public schools provide a diversity which our educational system would otherwise lack. They also give a spur of competition to the public schools—through which educational innovations come, both systems benefit, and progress results.

Should any single school system—public or private—ever acquire a complete monopoly over the education of our children, the absence of competition would neither be good for that school system nor good for the country. The non-public schools also give parents the opportunity to send their children to a school of their own choice, and of their own religious denomination. They offer a wider range of possibilities for education experimentation and special opportunities for minorities, especially Spanish-speaking Americans and black Americans.

Up to now, we have failed to consider the consequences of declining enrollments in *private* elementary and secondary schools, most of them church supported, which educate 11% of all pupils—close to six million school children. In the past two years, close to a thousand non-public elementary and secondary schools closed and most of their displaced students enrolled in local public schools.

If most or all private schools were to close or turn public, the added burden on public funds by the end of the 1970s would exceed $4 billion per year in operations, with an estimated $5 billion more needed for facilities.

There is another equally important consideration: these schools—non-sectarian, Catholic, Protestant, Jewish and other—often add a dimension of spiritual value giving children a moral code by which to live. This government cannot be indifferent to the potential collapse of such schools.

The specific problem of parochial schools is to be a particular assignment of the Commission.

In its deliberations, I urge the commission to keep two considerations in mind. First, our purpose here is not to aid religion in particular but to promote diversity in education; second, that non-public schools in America are closing at the rate of one a day.

Early Learning

In the development of the mind, child's play is serious business. One of my first initiatives upon taking office was to commit this Administration to an expansion of opportunities during the First Five Years of Life. That commitment was based on new scientific knowledge about the development of intelligence—that as much of that development takes place in the first five years as in the next thirteen.

We have established a new Office of Child Development in the Department of Health, Education and Welfare. I am now directing that Department and the Office of Economic Opportunity jointly to establish a network of experimental centers to discover what works best in early childhood education.

An experimental program of this nature is necessary as we expand our child development programs. The Early Learning Program will also provide us with a strong experimental base on which to build the new day care program, involving $386 million in its first full year of operation, which I have proposed as part of the Family Assistance Plan.

The experimental units of the Early Learning Program, working with the National Institute of Education, will study a number of provocative questions raised in recent years by educators and scientists:

—A study of language and number competence between lower and middle-class children shows a significant difference by the time a child is four years old, but the difference is said to become "awesome" by the time the child enters first grade. If this is so, what effect should it have on our approach to compensatory education in the early years?

—A study of poor children in Washington, D.C., conducted by the National Institute of Mental Health, indicates a decline in I.Q.s of infants between the ages of 14 and 21 months—a decline that can be forestalled by skillful tutoring during their second year. If this is true, how should it affect our approach to the education of the very young?

—Many child development experts believe that the best opportunity for improving the education of infants under the age of three lies not in institutional centers but at home, and through working with their mothers. What might we do, therefore, to communicate to young women and mothers—especially to those in or near poverty—the latest information on effective child development techniques with specific suggestions about its application at home?

The Future of Learning in America

The tone of this message, and the approach of this Administration, is intended to be challenging. America's educators have the capacity and dedication to respond to that challenge.

For most of our citizens, the American educational system is among the most successful in the history of the world. But for a portion of our population, it has never delivered on its promises. Until we know why education works when it is successful, we can know little about what makes it fail when it is unsuccessful. This is knowledge that must precede any rational attempt to provide our every student with the best possible education.

Mankind has witnessed a few great ages when understanding of a social or scientific process has expanded and changed so quickly as to revolutionize the process itself. The time has come for such an era in education.

There comes a time in any learning process that calls for reassessment and reinforcement. It calls for new directions in our methods of teaching, new understanding of our ways of learning, for a fresh emphasis on our basic research, so as to bring behavioral science and advanced technology to bear on problems that only appear to be insuperable.

That is why, in this field more importantly than in any other, I have called for fundamental studies that should lead to far-reaching reforms before going ahead with major new expenditures for "more of the same."

To state dogmatically "money is not the answer" is not the answer. Money will be needed, and this Administration is prepared to commit itself to substantial increases in Federal aid to education—to place this among the highest priorities in our budget—as we seek a better understanding of the basic truths of the learning process, as we gain a new confidence that our education dollars are being wisely invested to bring back their highest return in social benefits, and as we provide some assurance that those funds contribute toward fundamental reform of American education.

As we get more education for the dollar, we will ask the Congress to supply many more dollars for education.

In the meantime, we are committing effort and money toward finding out how to make our education dollars go further. Specifically, the 1971 budget increases funds for educational research by $67 million to a total of $312 million. Funds for the National Institute of Education would be in addition to this increase.

Nearly a century ago, Benjamin Disraeli advised Parliament that "upon the education of the people of this country the fate of this country depends." That is no less true in the United States today, where nearly one person out of three is teaching or studying in one of our schools and colleges and where the greatest social controversy of our generation has centered.

This Administration is committed to the principle and the practice of seeing to it that equal educational opportunity is provided every child in every corner of this land.

I am well aware that "quality education" is already being interpreted as "code words" for a delay of desegregation. We must never let that meaning take hold. Quality is what education is all about; desegregation is vital to that quality; as we improve the quality of education for all American children, we will help them improve the quality of their own lives in the next generation.

We must not permit the controversy about the progress toward desegregation to detract from the shared purpose of all—better education, and especially better education for the poor of every race and color.

That is why this Administration has committed itself to finding the reason—all other things seeming equal—why so much educational achievement remains unequal. We commit ourselves to the realizable dream of raising the American standard of learning.

Teachers and taxpayers alike must not accept the *status quo* in the process of teaching. We must make the schooling fit the student. We must improve education in those areas of life outside the school where people learn so much or so little. We must discover how to begin educating the young mind when it really begins to learn.

By demanding educational reform now, we can gain the understanding we need to help every student reach new levels of achievement; only by challenging conventional wisdom can we as a nation gain the wisdom we need to educate our young in the decade of the 70s.

Richard Nixon

The White House
March 3, 1970

Appendix B
Special Message to the
Congress on Higher
Education, March 19, 1970

To the Congress of the United States:

No qualified student who wants to go to college should be barred by lack of money. That has long been a great American goal; I propose that we achieve it now.

Something is basically unequal about opportunity for higher education when a young person whose family earns more than $15,000 a year is nine times more likely to attend college than a young person whose family earns less than $3,000.

Something is basically wrong with Federal policy toward higher education when it has failed to correct this inequity, and when government programs spending $5.3 billion yearly have largely been disjointed, ill-directed and without a coherent long-range plan.

Something is wrong with our higher education policy when—on the threshold of a decade in which enrollments will increase almost 50%—not nearly enough attention is focused on the two-year community colleges so important to the careers of so many young people.

Something is wrong with higher education itself when curricula are often irrelevant, structure is often outmoded, when there is an imbalance between teaching and research and too often an indifference to innovation.

To help right these wrongs, and to spur reform and innovation throughout higher education in America today, I am sending to the Congress my proposed Higher Education Opportunity Act of 1970.

In this legislation, *I propose that we expand and revamp student aid so that it places more emphasis on helping low-income students than it does today.*

I propose to create the National Student Loan Association to enable all students to obtain government-guaranteed loans, increasing the pool of resources available for this purpose by over one billion dollars in its first year of operation, with increasing aid in future years.

I propose to create a Career Education Program funded at $100 million in fiscal 1972 to assist States and institutions in meeting the additional costs of starting new programs to teach critically-needed skills in community colleges and technical institutes.

I propose to establish a National Foundation for Higher Education to make grants to support excellence, innovation and reform in private and public institutions. In its first year, this would be funded at $200 million.

There is much to be proud of in our system of higher education. Twenty-five years ago, two Americans in ten of college age went to college; today, nearly five out of ten go on to college; by 1976, we expect seven out of ten to further their education beyond secondary school.

This system teaching seven million students now employs more than half a million instructors and professors and spends approximately $23 billion a year. In its most visible form, the end result of this system contributes strongly to the highest standard of living on earth, indeed the highest in history. One of the discoveries of economists in recent years is the extraordinary, in truth the dominant, role which *investment in human beings* plays in economic growth. But the more profound influence of education has been in the shaping of the American democracy and the quality of life of the American people.

The impressive record compiled by a dedicated educational community stands in contrast to some grave shortcomings in our post-secondary educational system in general and to the Federal share of it in particular.

—Federal student loan programs have helped millions to finance higher education; yet the available resources have never been focused on the neediest students.
—The rapidly rising cost of higher education has created serious financial problems for colleges, and especially threatens the stability of private institutions.
—Too many people have fallen prey to the myth that a four-year liberal arts diploma is essential to a full and rewarding life, whereas in fact other forms of post-secondary education—such as a two-year community college or technical training course—are far better suited to the interests of many young people.
—The turmoil on the nation's campuses is a symbol of the urgent need for reform in curriculum, teaching, student participation, discipline and governance in our post-secondary institutions.
—The workings of the credit markets, particularly in periods of tight money, have hampered the ability of students to borrow for their education, even when those loans are guaranteed by the Federal government.
—The Federal involvement in higher education has grown in a random and haphazard manner, failing to produce an agency that can support innovation and reform.

We are entering an era when concern for the quality of American life requires that we organize our programs and our policies in ways that enhance that quality and open opportunities for all.

No element of our national life is more worthy of our attention, our support and our concern than higher education. For no element has greater impact on the careers, the personal growth and the happiness of so many of our citizens. And no element is of greater importance in providing the knowledge and leadership on which the vitality of our democracy and the strength of our economy depends.

This Administration's program for higher education springs from several deep convictions:

—*Equal educational opportunity*, which has long been a goal, must now become a reality for every young person in the United States, whatever his economic circumstances.
—*Institutional autonomy and academic freedom* should be strengthened by Federal support, never threatened with Federal domination.
—*Individual student aid* should be given in ways that fulfill each person's capacity to choose the kind of quality education most suited to him, thereby making institutions more responsive to student needs.
—*Support should complement rather than supplant* additional and continuing help from *all* other sources.
—*Diversity must be encouraged,* both between institutions and within each institution.

—*Basic reforms* in institutional organization, business management, governance, instruction, and academic programs are long overdue.

Student Financial Aid: Grants and Subsidized Loans

Aside from veterans' programs and social security benefits, the Federal government provides aid to students through four large programs: the Educational Opportunity Grants, College Work-Study Grants, National Defense Student Loans and Guaranteed Student Loans. In fiscal 1970 these programs provided an estimated $577 million in Federal funds to a total of 1.6 million individual students. For fiscal 1971, I have recommended a 10% increase in these programs to $633 million, for today's students must not be penalized while the process of reform goes on. But reform is needed.

Although designed to equalize educational opportunity, the programs of the past fail to aid large numbers of low-income students.

With the passage of this legislation, every low-income student entering an accredited college would be eligible for a combination of Federal grants and subsidized loans sufficient to give him the same ability to pay as a student from a family earning $10,000.

With the passage of this legislation, every qualified student would be able to augment his own resources with Federally-guaranteed loans, but Federal subsidies would be directed to students who need them most.

Under this plan, every student from a family below the $10,000 income level—nearly 40% of all students presently enrolled—would be eligible for Federal aid. When augmented by earnings, help from parents, market-rate loans or other public or private scholarship aid, this aid would be enough to assure him the education that he seeks.

The Secretary of Health, Education and Welfare would annually determine the formula that would most fairly allocate available Federal resources to qualified low-income students. Because subsidized loans multiply the available resources, and because the lowest-income students would receive more than those from families with incomes near $10,000, the effect would be a near-doubling of actual assistance available to most students with family incomes below $7,500.

If all eligible students from families with an annual income of $4,500 had received grants and subsidized loans under the existing student aid programs, they *would have received* an average of $215 each. Under our proposal, all eligible students from families of $4,500 annual income would be *guaranteed* a total of *$1,300* each in grants and subsidized loans. This would constitute the financing floor; it will be supplemented by earnings, other scholarships and access to unsubsidized loans.

Student Financial Aid: Loans

The Higher Education Opportunity Act of 1970 would strongly improve the ability of both educational and financial institutions to make student loans. Although most students today are eligible for Guaranteed Student Loans, many cannot obtain them. Because virtually all Guaranteed Loans are made by banks, a student is forced to assemble his financial aid package at two or more institutions—his bank and his college—and colleges are denied the ability to oversee the entire financial aid arrangements of their own students.

In order to provide the necessary liquidity in the student loan credit market, I am asking the Congress to charter a National Student Loan Association. This institution would play substantially the same role in student loans that the Federal National Mortgage Association plays in home loans.

The corporation would raise its initial capital through the sale of stock to foundations, colleges and financial institutions. It would issue its own securities—education bonds—which would be backed by a Federal guarantee. These securities would attract additional funds from sources that are not now participating in the student loan program.

The corporation would be able to buy and sell student loans made by qualified lenders—including colleges as well as financial institutions. This would serve to make more money available for the student loan program, and it would do so at no additional cost to the government.

The Secretary of Health, Education and Welfare, in consultation with the Secretary of the Treasury, would set an annual ceiling on these transactions. In fiscal 1972, I estimate that the N.S.L.A. would buy up to $2 billion in student loan paper.

Expanding credit in this manner would make it possible to terminate the payments now made to banks to induce them to make student loans in this tight money market. We would let the interest rates on these loans go to a market rate but the presence of the Federal guarantee would assure that this rate would result in a one to two percent interest reduction for each student. By removing the minimum repayment period we would not only enable students to pay back loans as quickly as they wish but we would make it possible for students to refinance their loans as soon as interest rates are lower.

We would continue to relieve all students of interest payments while they are in college but would defer rather than totally forgive those payments. This would be more than compensated for by extending the maximum repayment period from 10 to 20 years, easing the burden of repaying a student loan until the borrower is well out of school and earning a good income.

The added funds made available from these changes, which should exceed one-half billion dollars by 1975, would be redirected to aid for lower income students.

By increasing the maximum annual individual loan from $1,500 to $2,500, we would enhance the student's ability to avail himself of an education at any institution that will admit him.

Thus, the ability of all students to obtain loans would be increased, and the ability to borrow would be strongly increased for students from low-income families. The financial base of post-secondary education would be correspondingly strengthened. It is significant that this would be done at no cost to the Federal taxpayer.

Career Education

A traditional four-year college program is not suited to everyone. We should come to realize that a traditional diploma is not the exclusive symbol of an educated human being, and that "education" can be defined only in terms of the fulfillment, the enrichment and the wisdom that it brings to an individual. Our young people are not sheep to be regimented by the need for a certain type of status-bearing sheepskin.

Throughout this message, I use the term "college" to define all post-secondary education—including vocational schools, 4-year colleges, junior and community colleges, universities and graduate schools.

Any serious commitment to equal educational opportunity means a commitment to providing the right kind of education for an individual.

—A young person graduating from high school in one of the states that lacks an extensive public junior college system—more commonly and appropriately known as community colleges—today has little opportunity to avail himself of this immensely valuable but economical type of post-secondary education.

—A youth completing 12th grade in a city without an accessible technical institute is now deprived of a chance for many important kinds of training.

—A forty-year old woman with grown children who wants to return to school on a part-time basis, possibly to prepare for a new and rewarding career of her own, today may find no institution that meets her needs or may lack the means to pay for it.

We must act now to deal with these kinds of needs. Two-year community colleges and technical institutes hold great promise for giving the kind of education which leads to good jobs and also for filling national shortages in critical skill occupations.

Costs for these schools are relatively low, especially since there are few residential construction needs. A dollar spent on community colleges is probably spent as effectively as anywhere in the educational world.

These colleges, moreover, have helped many communities forge a new identity. They serve as a meeting ground for young and old, black and white, rich and poor, farmer and technician. They avoid the isolation, alienation and lack of reality that many young people find in multiversities or campuses far away from their own community.

At the same time, critical manpower shortages exist in the United States in many skilled occupational fields such as police and fire science, environmental technology and medical para-professionals. Community colleges and similar institutions have the potential to provide programs to train persons in these manpower-deficient fields. Special training like this typically costs more than general education and requires outside support.

Accordingly, I have proposed that Congress establish a Career Education Program, to be funded at $100 million in fiscal 1972.

The purpose of this program is to assist States and colleges in meeting the additional costs of starting career education programs in critical skill areas in community and junior colleges and technical institutes. The Department of Health, Education and Welfare would provide formula grants to the States, to help them meet a large part of the costs of equipping and running such programs, in critical skill areas as defined by the Secretary of Labor.

The National Foundation for Higher Education

One of the unique achievements of American higher education in the past century has been the standard of excellence that its leading institutions have set.

The most serious threat posed by the present fiscal plight of higher education is the possible loss of that excellence.

But the crisis in higher education at this time is more than simply one of finances. It has to do with the uses to which the resources of higher education are put, as well as to the amount of those resources, and it is past time the Federal government acknowledged its own responsibility for bringing about, through the forms of support it has given and the conditions of that support, a serious distortion of the activities of our centers of academic excellence.

For three decades now the Federal government has been hiring universities to do work it wanted done. In far the greatest measure, this work has been in the national interest, and the nation is in the debt of those universities that have so brilliantly performed it. But the time has come for the Federal government to help academic communities to pursue excellence and reform in fields of their own choosing as well, and by means of their own choice.

Educational excellence includes the State college experimenting with dramatically different courses of study, the community college mounting an outstanding program of technical education, the predominantly black college educating future leaders, the university turning toward new programs in ecology or oceanography, education or public administration.

Educational excellence is intimately bound up with innovation and reform. It is a difficult concept, for two institutions with similar ideas may mysteriously result in one superb educational program and one educational dead end. It is an especially difficult concept for a Federal agency, which is expected to be even-handed in the distribution of its resources to all comers.

And yet, over the past two decades, the National Science Foundation has promoted excellence in American science, and the National Institutes of Health has promoted excellence in American medical research.

Outside of science, however, there is no substantial Federal source for assistance for an institution wishing to experiment or reform. There is a heightened need in American higher education for some source for such support.

To meet this need, I have proposed the creation by Congress of a National Foundation for Higher Education. It would have three principal purposes:

—To provide a source of funds for the support of excellence, new ideas and reform in higher education, which could be given out on the basis of the quality of the institutions and programs concerned.
—To strengthen colleges and universities or courses of instruction that play a uniquely valuable role in American higher education or that are faced with special difficulties.
—To provide an organization concerned, on the highest level, with the development of national policy in higher education.

There is a need to stimulate more efficient and less expensive administration, by better management of financial resources that can reduce capital investment needs, and the use of school facilities year-round. There is also need for better, more useful curricula, while developing a new dimension of adult education.

There is a need to give students far greater opportunities to explore career direction through linking education with the world of work.

There is a need to develop avenues for genuine and responsible student participation in the university. Colleges of today and tomorrow must increase communications and participation between the administration and students, between faculty and students, where they are presently faulty, weak or nonexistent.

The National Foundation for Higher Education would be organized with a semi-autonomous board and director appointed by the President. It would make grants to individual institutions, to States and communities, and to public and private agencies. Its grants would emphasize innovative programs and would be limited to five years each.

A number of small, categorical programs presently located in the Department of Health, Education and Welfare—would be transferred to the Foundation. In addition to the more than $50 million now being spent in those programs, $150 million would be requested for the Foundation in fiscal 1972. Beginning with this $200 million budget, this Foundation would have the capacity to make a major impact on American higher education.

From the earliest times higher education has been a special concern of the national government.

A year ago I asserted two principles which would guide the relations of the Federal government to the students and faculties and institutions of higher education in the nation:

"First, that universities and colleges are places of excellence in which men are judged by achievement and merit in defined areas. . . . Second, . . . that violence or the threat of violence may never be permitted to influence the actions or judgments of the university community."

I stated then, and I repeat now, that while outside influences, such as the Federal government, can act in such a way as to threaten those principles, there is relatively little they can do to guarantee them. This is a matter not always understood. No one can be forced to be free. If a university community acts in such a way as to intimidate the free expression of opinion on the part of its own members, or free access to university functions, or free movement within the community, no outside force can do much about this. For to intervene to suppress, is by definition to suppress it.

For that reason I have repeatedly resisted efforts to attach detailed requirements on such matters as student discipline to programs of higher education. In the first place they won't work, and if they did work they would in that very process destroy what they nominally seek to preserve.

As we enter a new decade, we have a rare opportunity to review and reform the Federal role in post-secondary education. Most of the basic legislation that now defines the Federal role will expire in the next fifteen months. The easy approach would be simply to ask the Congress to extend these old programs. But the need for reform in higher education is so urgent, that I am asking the Congress for a thoroughgoing overhaul of Federal programs in higher education.

The Higher Education Opportunity Act of 1970 would accomplish this purpose. In addition, it would consolidate and modernize a number of other Federal programs that affect higher education. Through it, I propose to systematize and rationalize the Federal government's role in higher education for the first time.

In setting such an ambitious goal, we must also arouse the nation to a new awareness of its cost, and make clear that it must be borne by State, local and private sources as well as by Federal funds. In fiscal year 1972, I anticipate that the new programs authorized by the Higher Education Opportunity Act alone will cost $400 million more than the Federal government is presently spending for post-secondary education. If our goal is to be attained, there must be comparable growth in the investment of other public and private agencies.

The time has come for a renewed national commitment to post-secondary education and especially to its reform and revitalization. We must join with our creative and demanding young people to build a system of higher education worthy of the ideals of the people in it.

Richard Nixon

The White House
March 19, 1970

Appendix C
Memorandum for the President: Higher Education Options, March, 1970

Summary

The Higher Education Working Group included the following:

James E. Allen, Jr., Commissioner of Education
Lewis Butler, Assistant Secretary, HEW
Patrick Moynihan, Counsellor to the President
Herb Stein, Council of Economic Advisers
Lee A. DuBridge, Director, Office Science & Technology
Richard Nathan, Assistant Director, Budget Bureau
Edward L. Morgan, Deputy Assistant to the President
Jerome Rosow, Assistant Secretary of Labor

They have taken a dual approach to post-secondary education which involves dealing with new forms of *aid for institutions* on the one hand while at the same time expanding *financial aid for students* on the other.

Their proposals, together with arguments for and against each alternative and their recommendations, are set forth in the attachments. Briefly, they are as follows (with the options indicated):

A. Establish a New Financial Institution

(Enabling banks and colleges to expand the supply and availability of federally guaranteed student loans)

Options:

_____ Yes   _____ No

B. Student Aid

Restructure the Federal student subsidy program to concentrate more resources on low income students, with adjustments for family size, and number of students in college per family.

Options:

_____ 1. Limit to families with incomes of $10,000 or less (little additional money necessary).
_____ 2. Limit to families with incomes of $12,000 or less (approximate additional cost, $400 million).

141

_____ 3. Make no change in current subsidy programs. (Selection of this option will eliminate the need for the Financial Institution established in A above)

C. Establish a National Foundation for Higher Education

Options:

_____ Yes _____ No

Funding Level: Transfer $50 million in current programs and add new money in the amount of $100 − 150 − 200 million.

D. Community College Career Education Program

The two options presented are:

_____ 1. Provide State formula grants to fund *new programs* by matching State funds; basic decisions to be left to the States.
_____ 2. Provide project and exemplary program grants to fund approximately five model state programs at selected community colleges.

E. Funding

(New Money for 1972)

a) New Financial Institution   No new money (All private funding)
b) Student Aid
    Alternative (1)   Normal growth of existing program (from $633 million in 1971 to $806 million in 1972)
    Alternative (2) $400 million new money, *over and above* cost of Alternative (1).
c) National Foundation $100 − $200 million
d) Community Colleges $50 − $100 million

Recommendation

That you indicate your choice under each proposal submitted.

John D. Ehrlichman

New Financial Institution

Background:

1. Post-secondary educational institutions cannot make Federally guaranteed loans to their students because they lack sufficient liquid capital. As a

result, colleges cannot coordinate their students' financial aid arrangements and must refer them to banks, which may or may not have funds available for student loans.

2. Banks are often unwilling to make student loans, particularly to students from low income families.
3. Banks, particularly in tight money periods, must limit student loans because of inability to market those loans to others.
4. The 7% interest ceiling on guaranteed student loans, in this period of high interest rates, has made it necessary for the Federal government to pay a 2-1/4% special interest incentive to banks. This incentive has the effect of a subsidy for the students, but it is an unfocused subsidy and channels Federal funds to a number of middle-income students, while not specifically helping low-income students.

Proposal:

1. Submit legislation for the Federal government to charter a private financing institution similar to Fannie Mae, which would purchase student loan paper from colleges and banks and would finance these purchases by selling its own obligations in the open market. Total student loans purchased by the institution in FY '72 would run up to an estimated $2 billion. A detailed description of this institution is attached at Tab F.
2. Lift the 7% ceiling on student loans, permitting them to go to a market rate, thereby eliminating the incentive payments to banks.
3. Extend the period for repayment of guaranteed loans from 10 to 20 years and raise the borrowing limit from $1500 to $2500 per year.

Arguments Favoring

1. We are removing financial barriers to higher education for students prepared to invest in their own futures.
2. While increasing the *ability* of the student to pay for education, we are continuing to leave to colleges and states the decision as to how much the student *should* pay for his education.
3. We are increasing the range of choice available to the individual student by enabling students who are prepared to borrow to attend any institution that will admit them, rather than simply those they can afford.
4. We are accomplishing this through the private sector, and without additional burden on the Federal taxpayer.
5. By making it much easier for colleges themselves to make student loans, we are making loans more accessible to students and helping colleges to package all their students' financial aid from all sources.
6. Removal of the incentive payments to banks will save Federal dollars (about $50 million in FY '72) which can then be used to help needy students.
7. The mere fact of the Federal guarantee provides an effective interest subsidy of 1% − 2% for all students of whatever income level.

Arguments Against

1. We will attract private investment funds into student loans at a time when there are many other demands for investment dollars.

2. Letting loans go to market interest rates means that unsubsidized students may pay up to 9% or 10% interest rates in times of tight money, as against the maximum 7% that they pay under the present plan.
3. Colleges may be tempted to go into excessive debt.
4. Colleges may tend to raise their tuition because student ability to pay will be greater. (Some would argue that this is not a disadvantage.)
5. Those who favor universal tuition-free education may perceive this as a retreat by the Federal government. This includes many leaders in the higher education community.

Recommendation:

The Working Group unanimously recommends this proposal. It has also been approved by Secretary Finch, Secretary Kennedy, Director Mayo and Chairman McCracken.

_____ Approve
_____ Disapprove
_____ See Me

Student Aid

Background:

Presently the Federal government is providing four kinds of subsidies to students:

1. *Educational Opportunity Grants*
   Federal grants to low income students. Maximum annual grant of $1,000 per student, administered by colleges and universities. FY '71 budget request: $186 million.
2. *College Work Study Grants*
   Federal grants to lower-income students to pay their salaries for employment during the summer or the academic year. Administered by colleges and universities, which provide 20% matching funds. FY '71 budget request: $160 million.
3. *National Defense Student Loans*
   Federal government provides capital for colleges to make loans to students, mainly from families with less than $10,000 income. Students pay no interest while in school and only 3% after graduation with a 10-year repayment period. Administered by colleges, which provide 10% matching funds. FY '71 budget request: $142 million.
4. *Guaranteed Loan Program*
   Loans are made to students by commercial banks at a maximum interest of 7%. Federal government guarantees loans and pays interest while student is in college. Student pays interest after graduation and has 10-year repayment period. Federal government also provides a special incentive to lenders because of present tight money situation. FY '71 budget request: $145 million.

TOTAL FY '71 cost of the above four programs: $633 million.

Problems:

1. Under the guaranteed loan program, the Federal government is giving subsidies to all students from families with incomes up to $19,300 by paying interest on the student's guaranteed loan while he is in college.
2. By the 2-1/4% incentive payments to banks, we are, in effect, subsidizing all students regardless of income level.
3. Low income students who are eligible for Federal aid are not receiving funds because of budget restrictions.

Proposal: Student Aid

The Working Group proposes three alternative approaches:

1. Provide for subsidies to bring lower-income students up to the level of families with incomes of $10,000.
2. Provide subsidies to such students up to the level of families with incomes of $12,000.
3. Make no change in present programs.

Alternative 1—$10,000 level

Federal scholarships and subsidized loans would be used to enable all students from lower income families to have the same ability to pay for higher education as students from families with incomes of $10,000.

Arguments Favoring

1. Subsidies would go to students who need them most.
2. The Federal government would go out of the business of providing capital for direct student loans while providing the same student benefits through interest subsidies.
3. Although families with incomes of $10,000 and above would lose interest subsidies, they would now be permitted longer repayment periods.
4. The incentive for students to borrow at subsidized rates and use the proceeds for non-educational purposes would be eliminated.
5. We can fulfill this commitment with the present budget projections ($806 million by FY '72).

Arguments Against

1. We are taking away present subsidies from families with gross income of $10,000 and above. This means that an estimated 500,000 student borrowers who are presently enrolled and who would have been eligible for subsidies next year would not receive such subsidies on new loans.
2. Direct Federal loans to students are popular with Congress and with colleges and universities.

Alternative 2—$12,000 level

Identical with Alternative 1, except that subsidies would be provided to bring low income students up to the same ability to pay as students from families with $12,000 income.

Arguments Favoring

1. At $12,000 level, *620,000* more students would be eligible than in Alternative 1.

Arguments Against

1. This alternative would cost an added $400 million in FY '72.
2. Increasing the income level from $10,000 to $12,000 would increase the extent to which low income taxpayers are subsidizing higher income families.
3. The slight movement in income bracket does not justify this expenditure of funds.

Alternative 3—No change in Present System

Arguments Favoring

1. The present program is popular since almost all students are eligible for subsidies under the guaranteed loan program.
2. Any change in the direction of focusing subsidies on lower income students means that some higher income families presently eligible for assistance would not receive it in the future.
3. There is no great pressure in the Congress or in the colleges to change the system.

Arguments Against

1. The students who need help most are not receiving adequate aid under the present program.
2. If the volume of guaranteed loans is expanded through the financial intermediary but the present subsidy arrangements are not modified, the result could be a very large increase in the presently uncontrollable Federal expenditures for student subsidies.

Recommendation:

The Working Group recommends Alternative 1, with the exception of Jim Allen who prefers Alternative 2.

Approve: _____ Alternative 1 ($10,000)
_____ Alternative 2 ($12,000)
_____ Alternative 3 (No Change)
_____ See Me

The National Foundation for Higher Education

Pat Moynihan and Lee DuBridge propose that we submit legislation to create a National Foundation for Higher Education modeled in large part upon the

National Science Foundation. It would be a Federal agency, but separate and distinct from existing departments. The President would appoint the Director and the Board members, who would serve for fixed terms. The Foundation would have three principal functions:

a. To provide a source of funds for the support of excellence, innovation and reform in higher education; funds that could be given out on the basis of the quality of the institutions and programs concerned rather than on the bureaucratic (in the legitimate sense) basis of equal treatment for all comers.

b. To strengthen colleges and universities or courses of instruction that play a uniquely valuable role in American higher education or are faced with special difficulties. At the present time, this would include Negro and junior colleges and such special purpose programs as public administration.

c. To provide an organization concerned with the development of national policy in higher education, and to monitor the programs that derive from such policy.

Certain existing HEW programs could be transferred to such a Foundation. In time, other programs or agencies (such as the National Endowment for the Humanities) might also be merged into the Foundation. In addition, the Foundation would be provided with a substantial amount of "new money" of its own.

How It Would Work

The Foundation would not run programs or conduct research of its own. It would make grants of funds to institutions of post-secondary education and to state and local agencies. They would submit proposals to the Foundation's staff and board, which would assess them on the basis of their quality and their pertinence to national needs and priorities. Normally, the Foundation would fund only new or additional activities, and normally for a maximum of five years each.

Arguments Favoring

1. Federal activities affecting higher education are disorganized, fragmented, and lacking in any coherent policy or objectives. Twenty-five percent of the nation's higher education budget comes from Federal funds, but in a haphazard way that has simply grown up over the past several decades. This has produced large inefficiencies and disproportions. Somewhere in the Federal government there needs to be someone keeping an eye on this, pointing out emerging problems and trying to rationalize the flow of funds, particularly since enrollment will increase 50% in the 1970s.

2. The bulk of present Federal assistance goes for student aid and project research needed by individual Federal agencies. Except in science, there is little money for basic research or to support good ideas proposed by universities. The National Foundation would provide such funds.

3. A serious national threat—possibly the most serious—posed by the present

fiscal plight of higher education is the possibility of *loss of excellence.* In particular, the 50 to 100 great universities that produce the preponderance of American research, scholarship and graduate degrees are in financial trouble. A semi-autonomous Foundation is the only realistic approach to help sustain the extraordinary national resource found there. It would enable us to help identify and preserve excellence in a period when the Federal budget is likely to be very tight. The period has passed when we could afford to be sloppy.

4. It is widely held that higher education needs to be reformed—its curriculum, its management procedures, its organization and governance—and wholly new forms of higher education should be tried, but no Federal agency has the authority to fund such reforms and innovations. The National Foundation could exercise the wisdom and discretion necessary to promote such reforms in a way that no established agency could. It could strengthen selected Negro colleges. It could develop new curricula and programs in community colleges. It could fund special purpose programs in fields such as public administration, without supporting *every* institution or getting locked into permanent support of any program. It could administer its funds on the basis of the *quality* of the institution and the proposal, i.e., on the same basis as the National Science Foundation makes grants.

5. The Foundation can provide money while affording a certain insulation to the Administration itself. In many ways, members of the higher education community, chosen by the President, will be making the decisions about priorities and programs. It would be possible to recruit exceptionally able persons to staff such a Foundation and to provide imagination and rigor that are usually lacking in the bureaucratic agencies with their poorly administered, narrow categorical grant programs.

6. The Administration still needs to make some *money* gesture toward education. Funded at a reasonable level, the National Foundation for Higher Education would satisfy this need.

Arguments Against

1. If one of our problems is fragmentation of existing programs, we should not create yet another Federal unit in the field of higher education. Responsibility for policy should be concentrated—probably in HEW—rather than diluted further.

2. There is an elitist quality to a proposal that would assist leading universities. The large private universities are not as badly off as we think. Even if they are, they should solve their own problems. There would be more political impact from a program directed to all institutions.

3. If the great need in higher education is for reform and innovation, the Foundation is the wrong mechanism. It will tend more to confirm present practices than it will change them. It leaves too much of the initiative and responsibility with the educators, and in effect represents an abdication of Federal responsibility at just the time when that responsibility needs to be vigorously asserted.

4. With little additional money going into elementary and secondary education, this Foundation may tend to tip the balance of Federal investment toward higher education.

5. The Foundation might tend to dominate national thinking about higher education and inadvertently create a "new orthodoxy" in the field.

Recommendation

The Working Group is divided over the Foundation, but has no good alternative to propose.

Dr. Moynihan, Dr. DuBridge and Mr. Rosow strongly favor the foundation.

Mr. Stein and Mr. Nathan are, on balance, disposed toward it.

Mr. Butler and Commissioner Allen object to the Foundation, as does Secretary Finch.

_____ Approve: Establish New Foundation

_____ Disapprove

_____ See Me

Community College Career Education

Background:

1. Critical manpower shortages exist in skilled occupational areas, such as police and firemen, health aides, x-ray technicians, occupational therapists, and TV and electronics technicians.
2. Community colleges and similar institutions have a unique potential to provide programs in these and other manpower deficient fields. There are over 1,000 of these institutions in the United States. They enroll one-third of all college students, about one-fourth of whom are from low income families. Most are located in urban or suburban areas where manpower shortages exist.
3. Critical skills programs in community colleges often cost significantly more than general education programs, and thus receive special assistance from the Federal government at this time.

Proposal:

1. That the Federal Government support the development of *new* programs at community colleges and similar post-secondary educational institutions which provide career education in skilled occupations with critical manpower shortages.
2. Assuming that the proposal for a National Foundation on Higher Education is approved, one of the major purposes of the Foundation should be to support the development of high quality and innovative career education programs at two-year institutions.

Alternatives:

I: State Formula Grants

This program would have the following features:
a) Federal funds would be provided to States on a formula basis to support occupational programs at community colleges and similar institutions.

b) Only *new* programs which provide training in skills designated by the Secretary of Labor as those in which *critical manpower shortages* exist would be eligible.

c) Federal funds could only be used to support up to 50% of the *additional* costs of such programs over general education programs.

d) Federal funds could only be used for any critical skills program over a *three year* period, so that States would be encouraged to set up programs which ultimately can be financed without Federal aid.

e) The States would determine which programs and institutions met the eligibility criteria and whether to concentrate the funds in a few eligible institutions or spread them out broadly.

Arguments Favoring

1. This is a New Federalism program—it places responsibility upon the States.
2. It is focused on occupational areas of demonstrated need as determined by the Secretary of Labor.
3. It has incentives for quality and local participation, since only the additional costs of new programs would be supported and States and institutional matching funds are required.
4. It provides a logical and effective formula grant companion program to the project grant approach of the proposed Foundation.

Arguments Against

1. If a decision is made to fund the community college program at a relatively low level (less than $50 million), the funds may be distributed too widely among States and colleges to have any significant impact.
2. Some States do not yet have State agencies for community colleges and may not be able at this time to administer such a program with maximum effectiveness.

II: Project and Exemplary Program Grants

This alternative would support model programs designed to test whether and how community colleges can become a major focus for career education to meet critical skills needs. The Federal government, through project grants administered by the Office of Education, would be used for three purposes:

a) Grants to support the creation of *State administrative machinery* to channel Federal resources into community colleges and similar institutions (5% of the funds).

b) Funds to support a selected number (probably no more than five) *model State programs* providing aid to selected institutions to develop career education in critical skill areas designated by the Secretary of Labor (20% of the funds).

c) Project grant funds to cover a major portion of the extra costs of establishing and operating *model* critical skills programs at *selected* community colleges throughout the nation (75% of the total funding).

Arguments Favoring

1. This alternative provides the means to develop and test critical skills programs at selected institutions and determine if they have the capacity to do the job.

2. Manpower shortages vary widely in different geographic areas—this alternative allows funds to be concentrated in those areas of need and not dispersed widely.

Arguments Against

1. This alternative is not necessary, since the proposed National Foundation on Higher Education would administer the same type of project grants and model programs for community colleges.
2. It weakens the New Federalism thrust which is to strengthen State capacity for program development.
3. Congressional pressures to expand the proposed limit of five model State programs would be very hard to resist and could destroy the ability of the Federal government to concentrate funds and run model programs.

Recommendation:

The Working Group unanimously recommends Alternative I.

_____ Approve Alternative I
_____ Approve Alternative II
_____ See Me.

Funding Levels—Fiscal Year 1972

A. Since the new Financial Institution will be financed in the private sector, no new federal funds are necessary.
B. *Student aid:* Only if you elected Alternative II ($12,000 and below) are new Federal funds, in the amount of $400 million, required in Fiscal Year 1972.
C and D. *Foundation and Community Colleges:* $50 million of existing programs will be transferred to the Foundation. The remaining question is how much new money in Fiscal 1972 should be put into both the Foundation and the Community College-Career Education Program.

Given the minimums the group feels are necessary to retain credibility, namely at least $100 million in new money into the Foundation and $50 million into the Community College-Career Education Program, the six likely alternatives are set forth here.

Moynihan recommends $200 million for the Foundation and $50 million for the Community College Program. Budget recommends $100 to $150 million in the Foundation and either $50 or $100 million in the Community College Program.

Morgan recommends $150 million for the Foundation and $100 million in the Community College Program.

Recommendation

That you check one of the options listed on the following page:

Use of New Funds

	Foundation	Community Colleges Career-Education Program	Total
_____	1. $100 million	$ 50 million	$150 million (B.O.B.)
_____	2. 100 million	100 million	200 million (B.O.B.)
_____	3. 150 million	50 million	200 million
_____	4. 150 million	100 million	250 million (Morgan)
_____	5. 200 million	50 million	$250 million (Moynihan)
_____	6. 200 million	100 million	300 million
_____	See me		

1. *Nature of the Financial Institution*
   - It would be a Federally chartered, private, non-profit corporation established under proposed new legislation.
   - Its stated purpose would be to increase the ability of post-secondary educational institutions and financial institutions to make loans to students for their education.
   - It would perform this function by buying Federally guaranteed student loan paper from banks and colleges.
   - Like Fannie Mae, the new institution would obtain the funds needed by selling its own obligations in the open market.

2. *Structure of the Institution*
   - The President would appoint an interim board of directors to organize the corporation, the board to include representatives of educational and financial institutions.
   - Stock would be sold to educational and financial institutions to raise initial operating capital.
   - The stockholders would elect two thirds of the permanent board of directors; the President would appoint the other third.
   - The corporation would establish its own policies and procedures within the terms of its charter.

3. *Operations*
   - Students would borrow from their colleges or from banks.
   - The colleges and banks would take the student loan paper they did not wish to hold as an investment to the Federally chartered institution, and either sell it or obtain a loan with the student loan paper as collateral.
   - The funds obtained by banks and colleges from such transactions would be available to make additional loans to students.
   - Students would pay a rate of interest estimated at about one percent point higher than the rate at which the institution borrowed from the public.
   - This difference in interest rates would be enough to make the institution self supporting, and also to cover the costs incurred by banks and colleges in initiating and servicing loans.

4. *Limits on the Volume of Loans*
   - The Secretary of Health, Education and Welfare, in consultation with the Secretary of the Treasury, would determine how much the institution could borrow from the public subject to a Federal guarantee.
   - If the amount of money available to the institution is limited in a period of tight money so that it cannot meet all demands on its resources, loans to students having the greatest need would receive first consideration.
   - Funds available for lower priority loans would be allocated by auction in the manner of Fannie Mae.

Notes

Notes

Chapter 1
Advising the President

1. Thomas E. Cronin and Sanford D. Greenberg, eds., *The Presidential Advisory System* (New York: Harper & Row, 1969), p. xviii.

2. Arthur M. Schlesinger, Jr., *The Imperial Presidency* (Boston: Houghton Mifflin, 1973), pp. 222 and 408.

3. Thomas R. Wolanin, *Presidential Advisory Commissions* (Madison: University of Wisconsin Press, 1975), p. 124.

4. Ibid., p. 139.

Chapter 2
Stirrings and Startings

1. John L. Burns, Chairman, CED Subcommittee on Education of the Disadvantaged, "Education in the Ghetto," *Saturday Review*, January 11, 1969, p. 33.

2. Carl J. Dolce, "The Inner City—A Superintendent's View," *Saturday Review*, January 11, 1969, p. 36.

3. Kenneth W. Haskins, "The Case for Local Control," *Saturday Review*, January 11, 1969, p. 52.

4. Albert Shanker, "What's Wrong with Compensatory Education," *Saturday Review*, January 11, 1969, p. 61.

5. Nathan Glazer, "The New Left and Its Limits," *Commentary*, July 1968, p. 37. See also Nathan Glazer, " 'Student Power' in Berkeley," *The Public Interest*, Fall 1968, pp. 3-21.

6. Alan E. Bayer and Alexander W. Astin, *Campus Disruption During 1968-1969*, ACE Research Reports, vol. 4, no. 3 (Washington, D.C.: American Council on Education, August 1969).

7. Carnegie Commission on Higher Education, *Quality and Equality: New Levels of Federal Responsibility for Higher Education* (New York: McGraw-Hill, December 1968).

8. H.H. Jenny and G.R. Wynn, *The Turning Point* (Wooster, O.: The College of Wooster, 1972).

9. Quoted in William Safire, *Before The Fall* (Garden City, N.Y.: Doubleday, 1975), p. 647.

10. "Education for Excellence, Freedom and Diversity," in *Nixon Speaks Out*, Nixon-Agnew Campaign Committee, October 1968, p. 180.

11. Ibid., pp. 180-91.

12. *Special Analyses*, Budget of the United States, Fiscal Year 1970, Washington, D.C., Table J-4, p. 117.

13. *Federal Relations to Education,* Report of the National Advisory Committee on Education, Part 1, Committee Findings and Recommendations, Washington, D.C., 1931, p. 8.

14. Richard M. Nixon, "Special Message to the Congress on the Nation's Antipoverty Programs," February 19, 1969.

15. *Congressional Record*, March 25, 1969, p. E 2538.

16. Richard M. Nixon, "Statement on Campus Disorders," March 22, 1969.

17. Richard P. Nathan, *The Plot That Failed* (New York: John Wiley & Sons, 1975), p. 45.

Chapter 3
Elementary and Secondary Education

1. For additional reflections by the author on the Institute's origins, see "What the NIE Can Be," *Phi Delta Kappan* (February 1972); "The National Institute of Education," *The Yale Review* (Winter 1975); and "On 'The National Institute of Education'," *The Yale Review* (Spring 1975).

2. For an exhaustive account of this genealogy, see Lee Sproull, Stephen Weiner, and David Wolf, "Organizing an Anarchy: Belief, Bureaucracy and Politics in a New Federal Agency," unpublished manuscript, Stanford University, Stanford, Calif., 1975, especially Chapter 1.

3. "National Institute of Education: Preliminary Plan for the Proposed Institute," reprinted in House Select Subcommittee on Education, *Hearings To Establish a National Institute of Education*, 92nd Cong., 1st sess. Washington, D.C., 1971, pp. 518 ff.

4. For a stimulating account of Nixon and the parochial school issue, see William Safire, *Before The Fall* (Garden City, N.Y.: Doubleday, 1975), pp. 554-59.

5. Arthur E. Wise, *Rich Schools, Poor Schools: The Promise of Equal Opportunity* (Chicago: University of Chicago Press, 1969).

6. On the diverse rationales for such advisory commissions, see Thomas R. Wolanin, *Presidential Advisory Commissions* (Madison: University of Wisconsin Press, 1975).

7. Richard M. Nixon, "Statement About Desegregation of Elementary and Secondary Schools," March 24, 1970.

8. Ibid.

9. Ibid.

Chapter 4
Higher Education

1. *Toward a Long-Range Plan for Federal Financial Support for Higher Education*, U.S. Department of Health, Education and Welfare, Washington, D.C., January 1969, p. 22.

2. Carnegie Commission on Higher Education, *Quality and Equality: New Levels of Federal Responsibility for Higher Education* (New York: McGraw-Hill, December 1968).

3. Earl F. Cheit, *The New Depression in Higher Education* (New York: McGraw-Hill, 1971).

4. American Council on Education, *Federal Programs for Higher Education* (Washington, D.C.: ACE, 1969), p. 17.

5. Association of American Universities, *The Federal Financing of Higher Education* (Washington, D.C.: AAU, April 1968), p. 14.

6. National Science Board, *Toward a Public Policy for Graduate Education in the Sciences* (Washington, D.C., 1969), p. 38.

7. Quoted in Daniel P. Moynihan, "On Universal Higher Education," in Moynihan, *Coping: Essays On the Practice of Government* (New York: Random House, 1973), p. 288.

8. Carnegie Commission on Higher Education, *Dissent and Disruption* (New York: McGraw-Hill, 1971), p. 103.

9. Ibid., p. 165.

10. Roger A. Freeman, "Federal Assistance to Higher Education Through Income Tax Credits," in Joint Economic Committee, *The Economics and Financing of Higher Education in the United States*, 91st Cong. 1st sess., Washington, D.C., pp. 665-83.

11. *Priorities in Higher Education*, Report of the President's Task Force on Higher Education, Washington, D.C., August 1970.

12. *Toward a Long-Range Plan*, Appendix C, pp. 63-65.

13. *Quality and Equality*, pp. 27-30.

14. *Toward a Long-Range Plan*, pp. 32-33.

15. Ibid., pp. 31-32.

16. *Quality and Equality*, pp. 18-22.

17. Ibid., pp. 43-46.

18. Lawrence E. Gladieux and Thomas R. Wolanin, *Congress and the Colleges* (Lexington, Mass.: D.C. Heath, 1976), p. 73.

19. Daniel P. Moynihan, *Maximum Feasible Misunderstanding* (New York: The Free Press, 1970), p. 168.

20. Daniel P. Moynihan, "Policy vs. Program in the 1970s," in Moynihan, *Coping*, p. 272.

Chapter 5
Appraising the Nixon Legacy

1. *The Washington Post*, April 22, 1970, p. A-2.

2. See *The Washington Post*, March 7, 1970, p. A-14; *The New Republic*, Vol. 162, No. 12, March 21, 1970, p. 9; *The New York Times*, March 4, 1970, editorial page; Douglass Cater, "Back go a Stalemate in Education?" *The Washington Post*, March 15, 1970, p. B-1; and Joseph Alsop, "Nixon's Education Message May Be His Most Important," *The Washington Post*, March 16, 1970.

3. *Higher Education and National Affairs*, Vol. XIX, No. 11, March 20, 1970, p. 1.

4. Robert W. Hartman and Alice M. Rivlin, "Higher Education: An Analysis of the Nixon Proposals," in Subcommittee on Education, Senate Committee on Labor and Public Welfare, *Higher Education Amendments of 1970*, 91st Cong. 2nd sess., Washington, D.C., 1970, Part 1, p. 450.

5. For an excellent chronicle and analysis of the entire legislative sequence that culminated in the Education Amendments of 1972, see Lawrence E. Gladieux and Thomas R. Wolanin, *Congress and the Colleges* (Lexington, Mass.: D.C. Heath, 1976).

6. Daniel P. Moynihan, *Coping: Essays on the Practice of Government* (New York: Random House, 1973), p. 312.

7. Richard M. Nixon, News Conference, July 30, 1970.

8. *The Report of The President's Commission on Campus Unrest*, Washington, D.C., September 1970.

9. Quoted in *The New York Times*, September 30, 1970, p. 1.

10. Richard M. Nixon, Letter to the Chairman, President's Commission on Campus Unrest, on the Commission's Report, Washington, D.C., December 12, 1970.

11. Frank Newman and others, *Report on Higher Education*, Washington, D.C., March 1971. For a discussion of the linkage between the Newman Report and the revised foundation proposal, see Gladieux and Wolanin, *Congress and the Colleges*, pp. 77-80. For two markedly different perspectives on the administration's second foundation proposal, see Chester E. Finn, Jr., "Death of an Idea," *Change Magazine*, Vol. 4, No. 2, March 1972, and Russell Edgerton, "Viewpoint," *Change Magazine*, Vol. 5, No. 1, February 1973.

12. Gladieux and Wolanin, *Congress and the Colleges*, pp. 141-43, and Lee Sproull, Stephen Weiner, and David Wolf, "Organizing an Anarchy: Belief, Bureaucracy and Politics in a New Federal Agency," unpublished manuscript, Stanford University, Stanford, Calif., 1975.

13. Gary Orfield, "Congress, the President, and Anti-Busing Legislation, 1966-1974," *Journal of Law & Education*, Vol. 4, No. 1 (January 1975).

14. The Moynihan address may be found in Moynihan, *Coping*, pp. 285-313, and in W. Todd Furniss, ed., *Higher Education for Everybody?* (Washington, D.C.: American Council on Education, 1971), pp. 233-54.

15. Institute for Educational Leadership, *Perspectives on Federal Educational Policy* (Washington, D.C.: George Washington University, 1976), pp. 48-49.

16. Special Subcommittee on Education, House Committee on Education and Labor, *Higher Education Amendments of 1971*, 92nd Cong. 1st sess., Washington, D.C., 1971, Part 2, pp. 773-83.

17. Ibid., p. 648.

18. Charles B. Saunders, Jr., "The Student Aid Merry-Go-Round," *Change Magazine*, Vol. 8, No. 7, August 1976, p. 44.

19. Eugene Eidenberg and Roy D. Morey, *An Act of Congress* (New York: W.W. Norton, 1969), especially Chapter 8, and Stephen K. Bailey and Edith K. Mosher, *ESEA: The Office of Education Administers a Law* (Syracuse, N.Y.: Syracuse University Press, 1968), especially Chapter II.

20. *Congressional Record*, March 12, 1969, p. H-6103.

21. Daniel P. Moynihan, "Sources of Resistance to the Coleman Report," *Harvard Educational Review*, Vol, 38, No. 1, Winter 1968, p.25.

22. John Mathews, "Nixon Policy Takes on School Establishment," *Washington Evening Star*, March 4, 1970.

23. Lyndon Baines Johnson, *The Vantage Point* (New York: Holt, Rinehart & Winston, 1971), p. 209.

24. Stephen K. Bailey, "The Office of Education and the Education Act of 1965," in Michael W. Kirst, ed., *The Politics of Education at the Local, State and Federal Levels* (Berkeley, Calif.: McCutchan Publishing Company, 1970), p. 363.

25. Richard P. Nathan, *The Plot That Failed* (New York: John Wiley & Sons, 1975), p. 82.

26. Nixon actually fared even better with faculty members in 1972, winning 43 percent of their votes, but there was a wider gap in the latter year between professorial preferences and those of the general public, which reelected the Republicans with a 61 percent landslide. Everett Carll Ladd, Jr., and Seymour Martin Lipset, *Academics, Politics, and the 1972 Election* (Washington, D.C.: American Enterprise Institute, 1973), Table 8, p. 70.

27. Irving L. Janis, *Victims of Groupthink* (Boston: Houghton Mifflin, 1972), especially pp. 197-98.

Chapter 6
Education and the Presidency

1. Stephen Hess, *Organizing the Presidency* (Washington, D.C.: The Brookings Institution, 1976), p. 22.

2. Richard Rose, *Managing Presidential Objectives* (New York: The Free Press, 1976), p. 20.

3. For a sound examination of the tensions inherent in the OMB role, see Hugh Heclo, "OMB and the Presidency—the Problem of 'Neutral Competence'," *The Public Interest*, Winter 1975.

4. These observations owe much to the analysis in Hess, *Organizing the Presidency*.

5. For an elaboration of this point (and many others), see Aaron Wildavsky, *The Politics of the Budgetary Process*, 2nd ed. (Boston: Little, Brown, 1974).

6. Quoted in William Safire, *Before The Fall* (Garden City, N.Y.: Doubleday, 1975), p. 45.

7. For an informed discussion of this problem by one who favors creation of a separate education department, see Rufus E. Miles, Jr., *A Cabinet Department of Education* (Washington, D.C.: American Council on Education, 1976).

8. Janis discusses this problem at length and offers a range of imaginative remedies in *Victims of Groupthink* (Boston, Houghton Mifflin, 1972), especially pp. 209-19. See also Alexander L. George, "The Case for Multiple Advocacy in Making Foreign Policy," *The American Political Science Review*, Vol. LXVI, No. 3 (September 1972): pp. 751-85.

9. Hess, *Organizing the Presidency*, pp. 156 and 174.

10. Richard P. Nathan, *The Plot That Failed* (New York: John Wiley & Sons, 1975) especially pp. 81-94. See also Rose, *Managing Presidential Objectives*, especially pp. 145-169.

11. Arthur M. Schlesinger, Jr., *The Imperial Presidency* (Boston: Houghton Mifflin, 1973), especially Chapter 8, pp. 208-77.

Index

Index

165

About the Author

Chester E. Finn, Jr. received the B.A., M.A.T., and Ed.D. degrees from Harvard University. He served as staff assistant to the President of the United States from 1969 to 1971, as director of policy analysis at the University of Massachusetts from 1971 to 1972, and as special assistant for education to the governor of Massachusetts from 1972 to 1973. Dr. Finn went to New Delhi, India in early 1973 as Counsel to Ambassador Daniel P. Moynihan, and returned to Washington in late 1974 to become research associate in governmental studies at the Brookings Institution. He is the author or coauthor of two Brookings studies of higher education policy, and has written numerous articles and reviews for *Minerva, Commentary, The Phi Delta Kappan, The Chronicle of Higher Education, The Washington Post* and other periodicals.